RHODESIA FILE

Also by Kwame Nkrumah and obtainable from Panaf Books

BOOKS

- Towards Colonial Freedom
- Autobiography
- I Speak of Freedom
- Conciecism
- Neo-Colonialism
- Challenge of the Congo
- Axioms
- Voice from Conakry
- Dark Days in Ghana
- Handbook of Revolutionary Warfare
- Class Struggle in Africa
- The Struggle Continues
- Revolutionary Path
- Africa Must Unite

PAMPHLETS

- What I Mean by Positive Action
- The Spectre of Black Power
- Ghana: The Way Out
- The Struggle Continues
- Two Myths
- The Big Lie

Also available from Panaf Books

- Kwame Nkrumah – The Conakry Years: His Life and Letters Compiled by June Milne
- Kwame Nkrumah – A Concise Biography by June Milne
- Forward Ever by the editors of Panaf books

PANAF GREAT LIVES SERIES

- Nelson Mandela
- Patrice Lumumba
- Africa on The Move Ahmed Sékoutouré
- Sékoutouré
- Frantz Fanon
- Eduardo Mondlane
- Kwame Nkrumah
- Kanyama Chiume

KWAME NKRUMAH

Rhodesia File

The cover title is taken from a photograph of Nkrumah's handwriting as it appears on his Rhodesia File

Panaf

Panaf
London W1R 8PN

© Panaf

All rights reserved. No part of this
publication may be reproduced, stored
in a retrieval system or transmitted,
in any form or by any means, electronic,
mechanical, photocopying, recording or
otherwise, without the prior permission
of the publisher.

ISBN 978-0-901787-21-7

Abbreviations	viii
Chronology	xi
Introduction	1

1 THE RIGHT OF A PEOPLE TO RULE
   THEMSELVES   9

   Extracts from Nkrumah's Address to the fifteenth session
   of the UN General Assembly, 23 September 1960

2 SETTLER POLITICS   14

   Memorandum on 'Britain's responsibility in Southern
   Rhodesia' published by the Ghana government in 1963
   and addressed to the government and people of Britain

3 SOUTHERN RHODESIA: 'PARTICULAR
   AND URGENT ISSUES'   35

   Extracts from the Ghanaian delegate's speech in the UN
   Security Council, 9 September 1963

4 A NEW AFRICA   56

   Nkrumah's speech at the opening of the Summit Conference
   of the OAU in Accra, 21 October 1965; Resolution on
   Rhodesia carried unanimously

RHODESIA FILE

5 ONE MAN ONE VOTE   76

Views expressed by Nkrumah in discussions with British prime minister, Harold Wilson, in Accra on 31 October 1965; Ghana government statement issued on 31 October 1965; Message from Nkrumah to Wilson of 2 November 1965

6 MOCKERY OF DEMOCRACY   88

Ghana government statement on UDI, 11 November 1965

7 THREAT TO AFRICA   93

Nkrumah's press statement of 19 November 1965. Note dated 19 November 1965 from Nkrumah to heads of state of Congo, Zaire, Sudan, Uganda, Tanzania, Zambia and Guinea

8 CALL FOR ACTION IN RHODESIA   98

Nkrumah's Address to the National Assembly, Accra, 25 November 1965

9 GHANA BREAKS DIPLOMATIC RELATIONS WITH BRITAIN   118

Letter from Nkrumah to Harold Wilson, 11 December 1965; Message from Wilson to Nkrumah, 15 December 1965; Note from Nkrumah to Sékou Touré, 15 December 1965; Nkrumah's Address to the National Assembly, Accra, 16 December 1965

10 THE INADEQUACY OF ECONOMIC SANCTIONS   127

Ghana government statement of 10 January 1966

11 RHODESIA, AN AFRICAN VIEW   136

Article by Nkrumah published in *Punch*, 23 February 1966

12 'A SHORT, SHARP AND FIRM CAMPAIGN'   145

Letter to Harold Wilson concerning the Rhodesian situation written by Nkrumah in Conakry on 11 April 1966

CONTENTS

13 ZIMBABWE — 149

Extracts concerning settler politics and the liberation of southern Africa from the following books and pamphlets written by Nkrumah during the Conakry period 1966–71: *Axioms of Kwame Nkrumah* (Freedom Fighters' Edition); *Challenge of the Congo*; *Handbook of Revolutionary Warfare*: A Guide to the armed phase of the African Revolution; *The Struggle Continues*; *Class Struggle in Africa*; *Revolutionary Path*

14 APPENDIX I: UDI AND NEO-COLONIALISM — 169

INDEX — 200

ABBREVIATIONS

ECA	Economic Commission for Africa
OAU	Organisation of African Unity, founded in May 1963
PDG	Parti Démocratique de Guinée
UDI	Unilateral Declaration of Independence, declared in Rhodesia on 11 November 1965
UK	United Kingdom
UN	United Nations Organisation
UPP	United People's Party. Formed by the ten African members of the Rhodesian parliament after the 7 May 1965 general election
ZANU	Zimbabwe African National Union
ZAPU	Zimbabwe African Peoples Union

NOTE

The Introduction has been written by the publisher.
The publisher has also provided a connecting narrative with background information, which appears in italics at the beginning of each chapter.

CHRONOLOGY

1887		Gold Fields of South Africa Company formed
1888	11 February	British Commissioner made treaty of 'friendship' with Lo Bengula, chief of the Matabele. Lo Bengula agreed to make no treaties with other powers without the consent of the British
1888	30 October	Agents of Cecil Rhodes acquired from Lo Bengula all mineral rights of his kingdom
1889		Royal charter granted to Rhodes's British South Africa Company. First settlers in Southern Rhodesia
1890		Conquest of Mashonaland by British South Africa Company. Rhodes became prime minister of Cape Colony
1891		British protectorate established over Nyasaland (Zambia)
1893		Matabele rising defeated by British South Africa Company forces
1895		Matabele rose again. Defeated after heavy fighting
1904		12,506 settlers in Southern Rhodesia
1905		Gold exports rose to £1,500,000
1909		Gold exports £2,623,708
1911		£34,810 worth of tobacco exported. White population 23,606
1914		British South Africa Company charter renewed for ten years
1922		Referendum. Electors given choice of either affiliating with South Africa or of becoming

		self-governing. Vote of 8,774 to 5,089 in favour of self-government
1923	12 September	Southern Rhodesia became a self-governing British colony. Approximately 34,000 settlers.
1930		Apportionment Act. Established basis of European economic control of Southern Rhodesia: forty-eight per cent land allocated to Africans; fifty-two per cent to Europeans. The land reserved for Africans in general infertile, overcrowded and over-farmed
1953		Formation of the Central African Federation (Southern Rhodesia, Nyasaland and Northern Rhodesia)
1956		Population of Southern Rhodesia; 2,290,000 Africans; 176,000 Europeans: 13,000 Asians and mixed race
1959		Monckton Commission ruled that Southern Rhodesia was not a sovereign independent state
1961		New constitution in Southern Rhodesia bringing in electoral system removing safeguards for African interests. Rhodesian Front formed
1962		General election in Southern Rhodesia won by Rhodesian Front Party committed to policy of apartheid and break up of Central African Federation. ZAPU banned.
1962	October	United Nations General Assembly requested by a majority of eighty-one to two (with nineteen abstentions) that the UK secure the right to vote for all the people of Southern Rhodesia. Similar requests made on 14 October and 6 November 1963
1963		Meeting of UN Security Council called on the initiative of Ghana to examine Southern Rhodesian question. ZANU founded.
1963		End of the Central African Federation. Rhodesia's armed forces, previously under British command, handed over to settler government
1964	13 April	Resignation of prime minister of Rhodesia, Winston Field. Succeeded by Ian Smith
1964	16 April	Smith declared he did not believe there would be African majority rule in Rhodesia in his lifetime
1964	May	African heads of state in Addis Ababa re-

CHRONOLOGY

		quested UK not to transfer sovereignty to the foreign minority in Southern Rhodesia
1964	July	Commonwealth Prime Ministers Conference in London. Ian Smith not invited. Among resolutions passed on Rhodesia, no independence unless based on the consent of the Rhodesian people as a whole
1964	September	Discussions between Smith and Alec Douglas Home in London. Smith returned to Salisbury determined to convince UK that he had 'general consent' for independence based on the existing constitution (1961) and franchise
1964	14 October	Southern Rhodesian Independence Referendum Bill passed its final stage in Salisbury parliament
1964	20–26 October	*Indaba* of 622 chiefs and headmen at Domboshawa unanimously supported Smith government call for independence under 1961 constitution. UK government informed Smith that views of the chiefs would not be satisfactory evidence of opinion of the African population as a whole
1964	27 October	Wilson warned Smith that a unilateral declaration of independence (UDI) would have 'serious consequences' and be regarded as treason
1965	5 November	Referendum in Rhodesia. Voters asked if they were 'in favour of Southern Rhodesia obtaining independence on the basis of the constitution of Southern Rhodesia 1961'. Result: 58,176 Yes; 6,101 No; 944 Spoilt papers. Overall percentage of poll 61·6. Referendum boycotted by most 'B' roll voters, mainly Africans
1965	21 January	Smith rejected UK proposal to send an all-party parliamentary mission to Rhodesia
1965	22 February	Commonwealth Secretary, Arthur Bottomley and Lord Chancellor Gardiner arrived in Rhodesia to 'get a cross-section of opinion within the country'
1965	31 March	Smith announced a general election to take place on 7 May
1965	7 May	General election victory for Rhodesian Front with increased majority
1965	25 June	Opening of Commonwealth Prime Ministers Conference in London

RHODESIA FILE

1965	21 July	Visit of British Minister of State for Commonwealth Relations, Cledwyn Hughes, to Salisbury
1965	6 August	Visit of Commonwealth Secretary, Arthur Bottomley, to Ghana
1965	3 October	Smith and Lardner-Burke left Salisbury for final talks in London
1965	14 October	Wilson proposed that a Commonwealth prime ministers, mission should visit Rhodesia. Proposal rejected by Smith government
1965	21–26 October	OAU Summit in Accra. Resolutions on Rhodesia passed
1965	25–29 October	Visit of Wilson to Rhodesia. Proposal for Royal Commission to consider best means of consulting the people of Rhodesia on the question of independence
1965	5 November	State of emergency declared in Rhodesia
1965	7 November	Wilson proposed meeting Smith in Malta. Smith rejected proposal
1965	11 November	Unilateral declaration of independence by Smith government. New constitution published. Imposition by UK of economic sanctions against Rhodesia. Governor Sir Humphrey Gibbs announced the suspension of Ian Smith and his government. Announcement not published in Rhodesia due to censorship. Rhodesian High Commissioner in London, Brigadier Skeen, ordered out of UK
1965	12 November	Wilson declared UDI illegal and an act of rebellion. Resolution passed in plenary session of the UN condemning UDI and calling on UK to take the necessary steps to end the rebellion. Resolution passed by 107 votes to 2 (Portugal and Southern Africa). France abstained. UK did not participate in the voting. Smith announced that Governor Gibbs no longer held any executive powers in Rhodesia. ZANU announced the formation of a people's government inside Zimbabwe with HQ at Sikombela where its leaders were restricted
1965	15 November	Governor Gibbs stated that he remained legal governor and would not recognise either the illegal government or the 1965 constitution. Meeting of East African leaders in Nairobi (Kenya, Tanzania, Uganda, Zambia)

CHRONOLOGY

1965	17 November	C. W. Dupont sworn in as first 'acting officer' administering the Rhodesian government under the 1965 constitution. Zambia asked UK for troops to protect the power supply at Kariba. UK imposed oil sanctions
1965	19 November	Note sent by Nkrumah to heads of state of Congo, Zaire, Sudan, Uganda, Tanzania, Zambia and Guinea, calling for: 1. Urgent formation of an African High Command 'capable of being deployed against the illegal minority government of Southern Rhodesia'. 2. Treaty of Mutual Defence and Security between as many African states as possible. OAU Defence Committee met in Dar-es-Salaam. Chairman of the OAU Liberation Committee called on the Committee to recommend the way to implement the resolutions of the OAU Accra Summit of 1965 concerning Rhodesia. (See chapter 4.) No communique issued. Resolution of UN Security Council declaring UDI illegal and calling on UK to end the rebellion. All states asked not to recognise the illegal government of Rhodesia, and to break economic relations with Rhodesia
1965	25 November	Nkrumah called for UN to authorise the use of force to end rebellion. Military action preferably to be undertaken by African states. The UN to guarantee these states against attack by Portugal or South Africa. Nkrumah's readiness to commit Ghanaian forces strongly supported by Sékou Touré who was similarly prepared to place his forces at the disposal of the OAU, the UN or the UK for service in Zimbabwe
1965	30 November	Proposal from Ghana, Ethiopia, Somalia and Congo for meeting of OAU Council of Ministers to discuss Rhodesia
1965	5 December	OAU Council of Ministers announced total economic (including communications) blockade of Rhodesia. Nkrumah declared general mobilisation in Ghana, and the formation of a voluntary militia

RHODESIA FILE

1965	15 December	Ghana broke off diplomatic relations with UK and made it clear to UK government that this would mean withdrawal from the Commonwealth
1966	10 January	Ghana government statement declaring economic sanctions 'quite inadequate' to end rebellion and to bring majority rule to Rhodesia. Further call for use of force by African states, authorised by UN, since UK 'has ceased to have any control over the situation'
1966	24 February	Fall of CPP government in Ghana.

INTRODUCTION

Kwame Nkrumah began to assemble material for a book on Rhodesia several months before the unilateral declaration of independence (UDI) by Ian Smith's government on 11 November 1965. Nkrumah had by then written seven books, the last to be published being *Neocolonialism: The last stage of imperialism*. The manuscript of his seventh book, *Challenge of the Congo: A case study of foreign pressures in an independent state*, was in the hands of his publishers. Galleys had been corrected, and he awaited page proofs. But as always, even before publication, he was already working on the next project. This time there were to be two books. First, there was to be a manual of revolutionary warfare for African freedom fighters. Secondly, he resolved to write a book on the settler problem in Africa with special reference to Rhodesia. It was to be 'a case study of settler politics'.

When the 24 February 1966 coup took place in Ghana, a coup 'greeted so jubilantly in Salisbury by the settler government' Nkrumah had already assembled most of the material for both books. The manuscript of the manual of revolutionary warfare was left behind in his office in Flagstaff House, Accra when he departed for Hanoi on the Vietnam peace mission on 21 February 1966. According to Nkrumah this manuscript was 'handed over to imperialist and neocolonialist intelligence organisations by the military and police traitors who overthrew the CPP government three days later'. Nkrumah set to work on an entirely new manual shortly after arriving in Guinea in March 1966. This was published two years later by Panaf Books under the title *Handbook of Revolutionary Warfare: A guide to the armed phase of the African Revolution.* In this book, dedicated 'To the African guerrilla', Nkrumah had the freedom fighters of Zimbabwe very much in mind.

Most of the material which had been collected for the book on Rhodesia was also left behind in Ghana in February 1966. But a considerable number of official papers and documents were lodged in the Ghanaian embassy in Conakry, and these formed the backbone of the file on Rhodesia which Nkrumah began to compile shortly after his arrival in Conakry in March 1966. President Sékou Touré and the Parti Démocratique de Guinée (PDG) in an unprecedented expression of Pan-African solidarity had welcomed Nkrumah to Conakry on 2 March 1966 and proclaimed him co-President of Guinea. The Ghanaian embassy was closed and the ambassador's car and all the contents of the embassy put at the disposal of Nkrumah as representing the constitutional government of Ghana.

Throughout the five years of his stay in Guinea, Nkrumah followed developments in the Rhodesian situation with the keenest interest. At all times in close touch with freedom fighters, he deepened his knowledge by sending for and studying every report and account of the many aspects of the Rhodesian problem as they became available. For example, his file on Rhodesia contains a copy of a paper published by the African Studies Association of New York in 1968 entitled *Sanctions and the economy of Rhodesia.* Another is *The Rhodesian Front under sanctions.* There is a pamphlet: *Sanctions against Rhodesia: The economic background,* published by the Africa Bureau in London. Then there are copies of British government White Papers, one of them the *Report on Exchanges with the Regime since the Talks held in Salisbury in November 1968,* posted by his publishers, Panaf Books, at his request. Many other documents and cuttings from newspapers and magazines relating to Rhodesia, some of them annotated and marked by Nkrumah, are too numerous to mention, and it is not possible to reprint them in this book.

INTRODUCTION

The documents here published from Nkrumah's Rhodesia file are statements and writings on Rhodesia and problems relating to the liberation of southern Africa, written by Nkrumah himself. Ghanaian government statements and the speech of the Ghanaian delegate in the UN Security Council on 9 September 1963 (chapters 2, 3, 6 and 10) were certainly also prepared by Nkrumah. The final section 13, containing extracts from books and pamphlets written by Nkrumah during the Conakry period were not in his Rhodesia file, but have been added by the publisher. They summarise the views of Nkrumah after 24 February 1966 on the continuing struggle in Rhodesia, and the whole question of the liberation of southern Africa.

During the period of CPP government, 1957–66, Ghana became a focal point where African freedom fighters met and trained. Some were already engaged in armed conflict to end colonial rule. Others were struggling against settler minority governments or other reactionary regimes attempting to block the progress of the African revolution. All were welcome in Ghana where they were given every assistance possible. Training camps were set up and instructors experienced in guerrilla techniques were recruited from Cuba and elsewhere. To coordinate and promote African revolutionary objectives an African Affairs Centre and a Bureau of African Affairs were established in Accra.

Throughout his life, in private discussions with freedom fighters, in meetings and conferences, in speeches, broadcasts and in his many books, Nkrumah always emphasised the urgent need to think and to plan continentally. He viewed the Rhodesian problem in the context of the wider African revolutionary struggle to rid the continent of all forms of oppression and exploitation, and particularly in relation to the whole question of racist and minority governments in central and southern Africa. 'The authority to govern a state,' he said, 'should spring from the people, and the people's right to exercise these powers is based on the principle of one man one vote.' It was not a question of race or the level of education reached by the majority of the population: 'Wasn't the African, who is now considered unprepared to govern himself, governing himself before the advent of Europeans?' Still less was it a question of chasing all other races out of Africa: 'Settlers, provided they accept the principle of one man one vote and majority rule, may be tolerated; but settler minority governments, never.'

As it became increasingly apparent that the settler government of Rhodesia was moving towards UDI, Nkrumah did all in his power both to compel Britain to face up to her responsibilities, and to get African states to act together to assist the people of Zimbabwe. In the United Nations, at the Commonwealth Prime Ministers' Conference in London in July 1965, and at the OAU Summit in Accra in October 1965 he again and again proposed practical measures to prevent UDI. Once UDI had been declared he redoubled his efforts to bring an end to the Smith government. British prime minister, Harold Wilson declared that economic sanctions would bring down the Smith government in 'weeks rather than months'. But Nkrumah knew that they would be ineffective, and inadequate to deal with the situation. In a government statement of 10 January 1966 he declared: 'The government of Ghana regards it as hypocrisy for the United Kingdom government to ask African states to impose sanctions against Southern Rhodesia while at the same time the British government refuses to use the machinery of the United Nations to make these sanctions effective or to do anything to prevent them being flouted by Portugal, Britain's oldest ally, and South Africa, one of her principal trading partners.' He went on: 'The solution to the Southern Rhodesian question, therefore, in the Ghana government's opinion, lies in establishing majority rule in Southern Rhodesia at the earliest possible moment.'

On 25 November 1965, Nkrumah called for the UN to authorise the use of force, preferably by African states, to end the rebellion. Ten days later, on 5 December 1965, he ordered general mobilisation in Ghana, and announced the formation of a voluntary militia. In this action he was strongly supported by President Sékou Touré of Guinea, who declared that he was similarly prepared to place his forces at the disposal of the OAU, the UN or the UK for service in Zimbabwe.

Nkrumah set a time limit for Britain to end the rebellion in

INTRODUCTION

Rhodesia. When the time limit expired on 15 December 1965, Ghana in compliance with the OAU resolution agreed at the 1965 Accra Summit broke off diplomatic relations with Britain and announced that this step implied withdrawal from the Commonwealth. But only eight other African states honoured the OAU resolution and broke off diplomatic relations with Britain.

It was clear that Britain would not use force to end the settler rebellion, and that the imposition of economic sanctions alone would be insufficient to bring the Smith government down. In this situation, Nkrumah intensified his efforts to find an African solution. He had for many years campaigned for the setting up of an African High Command and for the creation of an Executive Council of the OAU so that African problems could be solved in Africa and by Africans. The Executive Council was to be a preliminary step towards the formation of an All-African Union Government. But his urgent appeals received insufficient support. Finally, in an attempt to assemble an African force capable of being deployed against the illegal minority government of Rhodesia, he called for the signing of a Treaty of Mutual Defence and Security between as many African states as possible 'to deal with the possibility of hostilities breaking out between any of the states subscribing to the Treaty and Southern Rhodesia, Portugal and South Africa'. At the same time he called for a meeting in Accra of the defence ministers of the Treaty states, to be attended also by military advisers and chiefs of staff. The coup in Ghana on 24 February 1966 put a stop to any further progress along these lines. The OAU meeting in Addis Ababa called to discuss Rhodesia broke up in confusion; Ian Smith's government breathed again; and the African revolution as a whole received the severest setback.

In Conakry, Nkrumah continued to do all he could to assist the liberation movements of Africa. It has been said that more freedom fighters passed through Villa Syli, Nkrumah's residence in Conakry, than through Flagstaff House in Accra during the whole period of CPP government. Nkrumah never tired in his efforts to mend splits among national liberation movements, since these only served the interests of imperialism and neo-colonialism. For example, he tried on many occasions to persuade members of the Zimbabwe African National Union (ZANU) and the Zimbabwe African People's Union (ZAPU) to unite. He held that differences between sections of national liberation movements as to the kind of society to be constructed after independence could be decided by the people themselves once they had been liberated. Until then, all should combine to defeat the common enemy.

On the question of violent or non-violent methods, Nkrumah was equally consistent, as the documents in this volume show. If revolutionary objectives can be achieved by peaceful means then there is no justification for armed struggle. But all methods, including the use of force, must be employed if peaceful methods fail to bring results. In the case of Rhodesia after UDI and the subsequent failure of economic sanctions to bring down the Smith government Nkrumah was more convinced than ever of the need to unify the struggle of the Zimbabwe people, and for All-African political and military co-ordination of strategy and tactics to complete the liberation of the continent. In the *Handbook of Revolutionary Warfare* he advocated the formation of an All-African People's Revolutionary Party (AAPRP) and an All-African People's Revolutionary Army (AAPRA) as a means towards the ultimate achievement of an All-African Union Government.

As will be seen from the following original synopsis, dated 7 December 1965, Nkrumah intended to write a comprehensive account of Rhodesia's history and of the events leading up to UDI.

SCHEME FOR A BOOK ON SOUTHERN RHODESIA

INTRODUCTION

This and the conclusion to be written later in the light of recent developments.

INTRODUCTION

CHAPTER I

History of Southern Rhodesia until 1953
Early history of Southern Rhodesia – Comparison with Ghana as the two gold producing countries of Africa in medieval times – The rise and fall of the Zimbabwe civilisation – The African system of rule in the nineteenth century – The Portuguese – Cecil Rhodes's invasion – Rule by the British South Africa Company until 1923 – Subsequent settler governments down to the formation of the Federation.

CHAPTER II

The Federation of Rhodesia and Nyasaland 1953–63
Connection between Zambia and Southern Rhodesia – Lord Malvern's plan for a settler government – The rise of the Dominion Party, the forerunner of the Rhodesian Front Party – African opposition to Federation – The reasons for the break up of the Federation.

CHAPTER III

The Economics of Southern Africa
The politico-economic connections between South Africa, Southern Rhodesia and the Portuguese colonies – The importance of Southern Rhodesia in the financial set up of Southern Africa. How neo-colonialism has operated there – A specific case study.

CHAPTER IV

The Nationalist Movements in Southern Rhodesia
The 1958 All-African Peoples Conference in Accra – Formation of ZAPU – The split in the nationalist movement – The relation of the nationalist movements with other liberation movements in Zambia, etc.

CHAPTER V

The 1961 Constitution of Southern Rhodesia
The object of the 1961 Constitution – The entrenching of racialism – The calculation of Welensky and Whitehead and why this went wrong – The story up to April, 1963 when negotiations for independence were begun by the Rhodesian Front.

CHAPTER VI

British policy in regard to the Independence of African States
General policy pursued by Britain in Africa – The Devonshire Declaration – History of other grants of independence with particular relation to the policy pursued in regard to Ghana.

CHAPTER VII

International repercussions of the Southern Rhodesian question
Question of Southern Rhodesia first raised by Ghana in the United Nations – Southern Rhodesia taken up by the OAU at its first Conference in Addis Ababa – The various United Nations and OAU discussions and resolutions on Southern Rhodesia – The 1963 Security Council Debate and the British veto – Discussions of the Rhodesian question at various Commonwealth Prime Ministers Conferences.

CHAPTER VIII

The Settler Revolt
The history of this revolt and the factors which led up to it – The various negotiations (British Bluebooks and White Papers, Command Papers 2073 and 2807) – Wilson's telephone conversations.

CHAPTER IX

Africa's reaction

CONCLUSION

To be written in the light of events at the time when the book is ready for publication.

Full use was to be made of Ghanaian state documents dealing with Rhodesia, and these were to form the connecting theme of the book.

The coup in Ghana, illness and the tragic death of Nkrumah in Bucarest on 27 April 1972, made the writing of the originally intended book on Rhodesia impossible. However, the selection of documents here published from his *Rhodesia File*, concentrating on the crucial UDI period, will it is hoped help in some small measure to alleviate the deep sense of loss to posterity of the greater, unwritten work.

Panaf Books
London
18 July 1975

1

THE RIGHT OF A PEOPLE TO RULE THEMSELVES

In the words of Nkrumah 'Rhodesia came into existence by trickery and force of arms'. By the end of the nineteenth century, the British South Africa Company, founded by diamond millionaire Cecil Rhodes, had conquered the people of Matabeleland and Mashonaland, and had begun the settlement and exploitation of the economic resources of Southern Rhodesia. In 1888, Lo Bengula, chief of the Matabele, signed away all mineral rights in his kingdom to Rhodes's company for a mere £100 a month. The following year, on 29 October 1889 a royal charter was granted to the British South Africa Company. The stated objects of the Company were:

a. *to extend the railway from Kimberley northward towards the Zambesi*
b. *to encourage emigration and colonisation*
c. *to promote trade and commerce*
d. *to secure all mineral rights in return for guarantees of protection and security of rights to the tribal chiefs*

Nine months later, a pioneer column consisting of some 200 settlers and police reached the site of Salisbury, the future capital of Southern Rhodesia, and built Fort Salisbury. Each man taking part in the expedition was promised not less than fifteen gold claims and a farm of 3,000 acres. By 1892 there were about 1,500 settlers prospecting for gold in Matabeleland, and acquiring land.

In 1893 and again in 1895 the Matabele rose and attacked the settlers, but were defeated after heavy fighting. European settlement continued, and by 1904 the white population had risen to 12,506. In 1905, gold exports rose to £1,500,000 and by 1909 to £2,623,708. In 1911, £34,810 worth of tobacco was exported. By this time there were some 23,600 settlers in Southern Rhodesia.

When the British South Africa Company's charter was due to expire in 1914 the electors of Southern Rhodesia were given the choice of requesting a renewal of the charter, or of bringing Southern Rhodesia into the Union of South Africa. They decided on a continuation of the status quo, and the royal charter was renewed for a further ten years.

In 1922, a referendum was held to decide between joining the Union of South Africa, or of becoming a self-governing colony of Britain. Some 8,774 voted for self-government, and 5,989 for entry into the Union of South Africa. The following year, on 12 September, the twenty-third anniversary of the arrival of the European pioneers at Fort Salisbury, Southern Rhodesia was annexed to the British crown and became a self-governing colony. There were then approximately 34,000 European settlers.

In the same year, 1923, the British government issued the Devonshire Declaration stating: 'His Majesty's government think it necessary definitely to record their considered opinion that the interests of the African native must be paramount, and if and when those interests and the interests of the immigrant races should conflict, the former should prevail.' As Nkrumah wrote: 'Since that date the whole history of Southern Rhodesia has consisted of the efforts made by the settlers to throw off this restraint and to obtain complete freedom to oppress and degrade the African population as they wished.'*

In 1953, the Central African Federation (CAF) was formed. It comprised the British colonies of Southern Rhodesia, Northern Rhodesia (Zambia), and Nyasaland (Malawi). The constitution of this Federation, enacted by Britain, gave the political control of its government to the European settlers. It is estimated that there were in 1956 about 2,290,000 Africans in Southern Rhodesia; 176,000 Europeans; and 13,000 Asians and people of mixed race. Approximately 48 per cent of the land was allocated to Africans, and 52 per cent to non-Africans, the latter occupying the most fertile areas.

* *Africa and the World*, Vol. 2, No. 16, January 1966.

THE RIGHT OF A PEOPLE TO RULE THEMSELVES

While Africans had fought against colonialist intrusion ever since Europeans first set foot on African soil, armed resistance had been comparatively easily suppressed, and foreign political and economic domination appeared likely to continue indefinitely. But African resistance which was always simmering just below the surface, re-emerged openly after the Second World War in the struggles for national liberation. A breakthrough was made on 6 March 1957 when the British West African colony of the Gold Coast became the independent state of Ghana under the leadership of Kwame Nkrumah and the Convention People's Party. There were at that time only eight independent African states. They were Ghana, Ethiopia, Libya, Tunisia, Morocco, Egypt, Liberia and Sudan. But the example of Ghana, and Nkrumah's vigorous Pan-African policies, accelerated the rate of political change in Africa.

In April 1958 Nkrumah called the Conference of Independent African States to meet in Accra. It was at this conference that the formula of one man one vote was adopted as an objective of the African Revolution. Eight months later, Nkrumah summoned to Accra the first All-African People's Conference. This was attended by delegates from sixty-two nationalist organisations from all parts of Africa. They agreed after long discussions to:

a. *work actively for a final assault on colonialism and imperialism*
b. *use non-violent means to achieve political freedom, but to be prepared to resist violence if the colonial powers resorted to force*
c. *set up a Permanent Secretariat to co-ordinate the efforts of all nationalist movements in Africa for the achievement of freedom*
d. *condemn racialism and tribalism wherever they exist and work for their eradication, and in particular to condemn the apartheid policy of the South African government*
e. *work for the ultimate achievement of a Union or Commonwealth of African States*

Within four years of Ghana's independence, eighteen other African states had gained their independence. The year 1960 became known as 'Africa Year' because in that year alone so many African states obtained their political freedom. In that year also, on 30 June, Ghana became a republic. In the new republican constitution two provisions were of basic importance:

a. *the proclaiming of the principle of one man one vote*
b. *the conferring of powers providing for the surrender of Ghana's sovereignty, in whole or in part, if at any time Ghana joined a Union of African States*

Three months later, on 23 September 1960, Nkrumah addressed the General Assembly of the United Nations in New York. His speech left the world in no doubt as to the main objectives of the African Revolution, and particularly independent Africa's policies regarding the problem of settler minority governments.

Extracts from Nkrumah's Address to the fifteenth session of the General Assembly of the United Nations, 23 September 1960

The great tide of history flows and as it flows it carries to the shores of reality the stubborn facts of life and man's relations, one with another. One cardinal fact of our time is the momentous impact of Africa's awakening upon the modern world. The flowing tide of African nationalism sweeps everything before it and constitutes a challenge to the colonial powers to make a just restitution for the years of injustice and crime committed against our continent.

But Africa does not seek vengeance. It is against her very nature to harbour malice. Over two hundred millions of our people cry out with one voice of tremendous power – and what do we say? We do not ask for death for our oppressors. We do not pronounce wishes of ill-fate for our slavemasters. We make an assertion of a just and positive demand, our voice booms across the oceans and mountains, over the hills and valleys, in the desert places and through the vast expanse of mankind's habitation, and it calls out for the freedom of Africa: Africa wants her freedom. Africa must be free. It is a simple call, but it is also a signal lighting a red warning to those who would tend to ignore it.

. . . . . .

The problem of Africa, looked at as a whole, is a wide and diversified one. But its true solution lies in the application of one

THE RIGHT OF A PEOPLE TO RULE THEMSELVES

principle, namely, the right of a people to rule themselves. No compromise can affect this cardinal and fundamental principle, and the idea that when a handful of settlers acquires a living space on our continent the indigenes must lose this right, is not only a serious travesty of justice, but is also a woeful contradiction of the very dictates of history.

Out of a total African population of over two hundred and thirty million people some three per cent are of non-African origin. To suppose that such a small minority could in any other continent produce acute political difficulties would be unthinkable. Yet such is the subconscious feeling of certain European settlers in Africa that to them the paramount issue in Africa is not the welfare of the ninety-seven per cent but rather the entrenchment of the rights of the three per cent of this European settler minority in Africa.

To these minority settlers a solution seems impossible unless what they describe as 'justice' is done to the foreign three per cent. Justice, they say, must be done to this group irrespective of whether it means that injustice continues to be done to the remaining inhabitants. I believe that a reasonable solution can be found to the African problem which would not prejudice the rights of the minorities on the continent. No effective solution, however, can be found, if political thinking in regard to a solution begins with the rights of the three per cent and only considers the rights of the ninety-seven per cent within the framework which is acceptable to the rest.

2

SETTLER POLITICS

During the period of the Central African Federation, Ian Smith's Rhodesian Front Party was born. It was initially called the 'Dominion Party' since it aimed to create an independent European dominion to include the copper belt areas of Zambia and Katanga. In 1962, the Dominion Party then renamed the Rhodesian Front Party, won the settler general election in Southern Rhodesia.

Under the 1961 constitution the right to vote in Southern Rhodesia was based on a complex scale of educational, financial and property ownership qualifications, so that in effect political power remained firmly in the hands of the minority, settler community. The electorate was divided into two categories, the 'A' roll and the 'B' roll. Qualifications for the 'A' roll to elect fifty out of the sixty-five members of parliament were as follows:

a. an income of £792 or ownership of property valued at £1,650
b. an income of £528 or ownership of property valued at £1,100 and completion of a course of primary education
c. an income of £330 or ownership of property valued at £550 and four years' secondary education
d. appointment as a chief or headman

Qualifications for the 'B' roll to elect only fifteen members were:

a. an income of £264 or ownership of property valued at £495
b. an income of £132 or ownership of property valued at £275 and two years' secondary education

c. 30 years of age and an income of £132 or ownership of property valued at £275 and primary education
d. 30 years of age and an income of £198 or ownership of property valued at £385
e. kraal heads with a following of twenty or more heads of families
f. ministers of religion

The numbers of registered voters in August 1964 were:

	'A' roll	'B' roll
Africans	2,263	10,466
Europeans	89,278	608
Asians	1,231	114
Coloureds	1,308	176
	94,080	11,364

In 1965, the Smith government offered to lower the qualifications for the 'B' roll to enfranchise most of the African population. But without an increase in the fifteen members of parliament to be elected by 'B' roll voters the offer would not have threatened the continued political domination of the settler minority.

Educational qualifications for the franchise were difficult, if not unattainable, for a large proportion of Africans. African education was neither compulsory nor free, and government expenditure on it was directed mainly to primary schools. Secondary and post-secondary education was mainly for non-Africans. Estimated government expenditure per pupil for 1965/66 amounted to £10 per African and £100 per non-African child. In view of the settler government's educational policies, and the general impoverishment of the African population, many Africans failed to complete even a primary course, and few went on to secondary and post-secondary education.

Similarly, the income qualification was unattainable in practice for the majority of Africans. In 1963, according to the Central Statistical Office in Rhodesia, only 41 per cent of the total African labour force earned over the minimum amount to qualify for the 'B' roll. But this earnings qualification was in addition to a requirement of either two years secondary education or complete primary education. No official estimates were made to show how many Africans possessed both these financial and educational qualifications.

As far as property qualifications were concerned, some 50 per cent of the African adult population was engaged in agriculture in the Tribal Trust lands. This land, farmed on a communal tenure basis, did not therefore provide Africans with property requirements necessary to qualify for the franchise.

In theory, the 1961 constitution of Southern Rhodesia provided for a gradual advancement of the African voter from the 'B' to the 'A' roll. But in practice, progress was negligible since little improvement was made in the position of the majority of Africans as regards education, land tenure, and general standard of living.

In October 1962, the United Nations General Assembly requested by a majority of eighty-one to two (with nineteen abstentions) that Britain secure the right to vote for all the people of Southern Rhodesia. Similar requests were made on 14 October and 6 November 1963, it being held that it was clearly Britain's responsibility to see that the African population of the colony of Southern Rhodesia were enfranchised. The following Memorandum on Southern Rhodesia published by the Ghana government in 1963 provides a summary of the background to the Southern Rhodesian problem at that time, and was largely instrumental in convincing members of the UN Security Council that it was the urgent duty of Britain to secure conditions for representative government in the colony.

Memorandum on Southern Rhodesia published by the Ghana government in 1963, and addressed to the government and people of Britain. In the words of the Preface: 'Its purpose is to spell out in clear and unequivocal language the position of the people and government of Ghana, which is in close accord with the stand taken by the rest of Africa on the grave issue which the Southern Rhodesian question raises. Briefly stated, this position is that the government of Great Britain has an inescapable responsibility in directing the evolution of the European settler colony of Southern Rhodesia toward an independent government, with a universal franchise, based on the oft-proclaimed British principle of one man one vote.'

The African people are the rightful owners of the land of Southern Rhodesia. Because of a European settler policy, maintained with the implicit or explicit support of successive British governments, the Africans have been systematically deprived of their land. Moreover, all constitutional means of access to political power – which is necessary to right the social and economic wrongs brought about by this policy have been removed from them. Shorn of property rights, shorn, too, of political rights by which the former might be restored, the African majority has one of two alternatives. It must either accept a future of unremitting poverty, or it must set itself upon the path to revolution. There is an enormous disparity in Southern Rhodesia, between the quantity and quality of land occupied by Europeans and Africans. The best land – farms and reserves – is allotted to Europeans. The worst patches have been allotted to the Africans. There are only 223,000 Europeans as against 3,690,000 Africans. That is to say, the African population is sixteen times greater than the European population. But the total acreage of land (41 million) occupied by Europeans is approximately the same as that (44 million) occupied by Africans. The European farms, therefore, are vast in size. Approximately 2 per cent of this land is devoted to farms of less than 1,000 acres. Over 33 per cent of it consists of farms of more than 20,000 acres.

More than three million of the Africans live on the land. They either cultivate their own, tiny, unproductive plots at subsistence or below subsistence levels, or they work as labourers for the European farmers. The overall tendency, therefore, in the apportionment of land has been either to dispossess the African farmer entirely or to relegate him to inferior and smaller holdings. And, in conjunction with this tendency, the dispossessed have been either assimilated as cheap farm labour on European land or have been funnelled into the towns as cheap domestic or unskilled labour. One may readily see why land apportionment is one of the most important political issues in the colony today.

The present distribution of land in Southern Rhodesia can in no way be construed as a mere result of the operation of a free market. Until 1887 the area now known as Southern Rhodesia was chiefly occupied by the Matabele people. In that year, an agent of Cecil Rhodes 'diddled' – as J. Rogaly puts it* – the Matabele chief, Lo Bengula, out of all mineral rights in his

* 'Rhodesia: Britain's Deep South', The Economist Intelligence Unit, 1962.

kingdom in exchange for £100 monthly, plus rifles and ammunition. In 1889, Rhodes' British South Africa Company – which received the aforementioned mineral rights – was granted a royal charter. This company, with its own army of freebooters, conquered Mashonaland in 1890. In 1893 the company picked a quarrel with the Matabele and crushed them too. In short, the present configuration of land ownership in the colony is the direct result of trickery, conquest and expropriation. It is not an historical or economic accident.

It was Rhodes' purpose to create a new European dominion in the heart of Africa. The subsequently conquered territory was known to possess an agricultural potential, mineral resources and climate eminently suitable for this purpose. Those men who participated in the military expedition of 1890 knew that immense wealth would be theirs if their mission succeeded. Each would be given a minimum of 15 gold claims, 3,000 acres of farm land, and an enormous reserve of exploitable manpower, represented by Mashona and Matabele labour.*

Today, the economic and political structure of the colony sharply reflect the original purpose which its establishment was intended to serve. There is a substantial European settler community. And it is this community which controls the land, mineral wealth and industry. In order to secure these privileges, they also control the government. The Apportionment Act of 1930, which has been referred to as 'the Magna Carta of the European', established solidly and legally the basis of European economic control. In this act, 48 per cent of the land was allocated to the African population and 52 per cent to the European. In justification of this division, the then senior official of the Native Affairs Department testified before the Carter Commission (whose report laid the foundation for the Act) in the following terms:

> 'We,' he said, 'are in this country because we represent a higher civilization, because we are better men. It is our only excuse for having taken the land.'

* P. Kheatley, *The Politics of Partnership*, Penguin, 1963, pp 26–27.

The proportions of land reserved to the two races was revised in 1962, but not substantially.

The land reserved for the Africans, by contrast with that of the Europeans, is poor and infertile, overcrowded and overfarmed. Two million out of the total African population live on the reservations, where the soil, already poor, is further exhausted through inevitably excessive cultivation. Even on the basis of subsistence agriculture, these reservations can no longer support the people. Further, they lack roads, irrigation and running water. Health and educational facilities are rudimentary. African men are thus forced into the towns and on to European farms, leaving a vastly disproportionate number of women and children on the reservations. Over one million Africans now work on European farms. They are hired on terms which necessitate long separations from their families. Housing conditions are miserable and wages grossly inadequate.

Because of the limited amount of arable land available within the African reserves, the farmer's allocation is often reduced by $\frac{1}{2}$ to $\frac{1}{3}$ of the permitted legal maximum (6 acres). To this gross economic deprivation must be added an equally gross administrative tyranny, for the 'native commissioners' of the colonial government can, at their discretion, revoke a grant of land for bad farming and remove the farmer from one farm to another.

It might appear that the 44 million acres of land now allotted to the African population is sufficient. But if the former figure were averaged out over the latter, one would only be left with 22 acres per person. Much of this acreage would be fit for grazing, but only a far smaller proportion for farming. But the iniquity in this allocation becomes glaring when one considers that the minimum allocation of land to a European immigrant is 750 acres; indeed it is not unusual for a European to be granted as much as 3,000 acres of land. This disproportionate allotment is justified in the specious grounds that, agricultural conditions in Southern Rhodesia being what they are, farms of a smaller size would not be worth maintaining economically. If farms under 750 acres broad are uneconomical, then it cannot require much thought, or human sympathy, to imagine the misery which must be borne by Africans confined to less than six.

Despite the enormous disabilities from which, as may be seen, the African farmer suffers, he nevertheless produces a small and limited range and quantity of goods for the commercial market. But even when he does, legislation has been enacted which places a further, inequitable burden upon him in respect of his settler competitors. The Tobacco Marketing Board for example, effectively reserves the growing of high grade Virginia tobaccos which bring the highest return, to European farmers alone. Maize is a staple crop in Rhodesia, and here also, legislation places a disability upon the African grower. Generally, his crops will not be accepted as of equal quality, but even when they are, he will receive only 25*s*. 6*d*. per bag, after a series of special deductions are made, while the European producer will be paid 38*s*. clear – without deductions. Again, the Southern Rhodesian Cold Storage Commission, without respect to the quality of African cattle, will only buy from European ranchers. These examples only serve to show that even when the African can produce, and when his products are as good as those of Europeans, he will, frequently and as a matter of deliberate policy, be refused the right of sale, or be paid significantly less than settler competitors.

The effect of these policies, enshrined in law, is further to secure the fixedly subordinate and impoverished state of the African. Such a policy is considered a necessary means of protecting the entrenched rights – economic and political – of the settlers.

Dispossession of the African farmer and the discriminatory treatment of his produce, however, form only – although the basic – aspect of European supremacist policy in Southern Rhodesia. Other aspects of this policy consist in excessive taxation of Africans; indirect, but effective, compulsion requiring that they work for Europeans as migrant labourers; the calculated depression of their wages to a fraction of that paid Europeans; their virtual exclusion from the professions; their exclusion from property, either as owners or as renters in central urban areas; discriminatory treatment in shops, hotels and elsewhere; the demand that they carry identity cards which are more or less equivalent to South African passes; and the severely limited educational opportunities for Africans, as compared with entirely free secondary education for settlers.

In regard to taxation, its chief purpose was, from as early as 1896 (when the first hut tax was imposed) not only to secure revenue for the British South Africa Company (which was then the government) but also to force from the reservations, and to make available to Europeans, African labour. In 1902, this tax was doubled from 10s. to £1, representing then an African labourer's wages of a month. The essential features of the system remain, and due to the government's tax policy, coupled with the insufficiency of available land, large numbers of male Africans are forced to seek work in areas exclusively reserved for Europeans.

These labourers, in both town and country, are excluded from the more remunerative jobs, especially in industry, and their salaries average under one-tenth the wages of Europeans. Moreover, they have virtually no civil rights. To live outside the reservations, they must have their employers' consent. If dismissed, they are liable to prosecution as vagrants. If they *quit* their jobs, they can be, and, indeed, usually are, imprisoned and subsequently compelled to resume the job they left.

Even on the reserves, however, the lives of Africans are controlled in the minutest detail by native commissioners who act as chiefs of police, agricultural controllers and judges – all in one – and thus exercise virtually absolute power. Still, life in the 'location', as it is called, at least from the point of rights, is worse. The African labourer may only have a visitor to stay in his lodging for two weeks. He may not be out of doors after 9 p.m. For African domestic servants, conditions are worse still. They are invariably refused permission to have their children live with them. There are no schools for their children, in any case.

One might continue, in great detail, to elaborate upon these methods, created and operated by the Southern Rhodesian government, the purpose and effect of which is to assure the subordination and dispossession of the African people. But at the heart of the matter is the irreducible question of land. Its disposition is the most crucial issue in Southern Rhodesia. Other aspects of the colony's repressive African policy are built upon it. Since the days of the British South African Company the land preserved for the European settlers has been the best – with the best soil and ample rainfall, and the most adequate communications by road and rail.

Not only is the settler's land the best, but he generally has far more than he needs or can actively cultivate. One writer, in remarking upon the strikingly low average of land utilisation and productivity by the settler population, wrote that 'Some of the best agricultural scientists in the country will tell you that a careful farmer could do as well on seventy acres as many Rhodesians do on 2,000 . . .'* In fact, only a small proportion of arable land held by Europeans is under cultivation. In 1957, the proportion was estimated – by a select committee of the colonial legislature – at *between 3 per cent and 4 per cent*. Much of the land is not being farmed or is held by absentee landlords in Britain. In 1962, the percentage of European land under cultivation fell still further.

Not only is the land in European possession under-cultivated, but large tracts of entirely unoccupied land, approximately eight million acres, are reserved for future European use, and denied presently to Africans – despite the acute land hunger among the African population. This, too, forms part of a concerted policy. Irrespective of whether the land is farmed or not, it is felt to be financially and politically essential for the European farmer to deny land to the African inhabitants. To act otherwise would promote a higher level of agricultural production among Africans and provide them with the basis for successful competition with European farmers. Further, if a class of prosperous African farmers were to emerge, the present availability of cheap African labour for European mines, industry

* Professor T. R. M. Creighton, *The Anatomy of Partnership*. Faber and Faber, 1960, p. 146.

and large scale farms would be seriously curtailed. And, finally, if the land available to European settlement were restricted, the terms of settlement would be less attractive because the type of farming demanded would be qualitatively higher, and one's ability to earn a profit more risky, the result being a diminished appeal to prospective European immigrants.

Herein lies the key to the entire politico-economic situation. Very attractive conditions for European immigration are created on the basis of depriving the African of such political expression and rights as would enable him, through the means of constitutional procedure, to recoup or balance his losses. Further, to deprive the African, *as such*, of rights to property and political expression, can only be done on the basis of racialist assumptions – which, in respect of formal government pronouncements, are tacit, but which, in the case of settler practices and opinions, are usually blatant and explicit.

A calculated effort has been made to deprive Africans of their political rights. The effect of such deprivation is to perpetuate the economically advantageous position of Europeans. One of the most essential of political rights is the vote. In regard to it, the present British Prime Minister declared in the House of Commons on November 28th, 1963: 'I think there is no dispute that the Southern Rhodesian franchise is in accordance with the principle of majority rule.'

But Mr Humphry Berkeley, M.P. (Conservative) in the *Observer* of March 1st, 1964, wrote: 'It is unlikely that under the present constitution the Africans will gain majority rule in less than thirty years. Majority rule,' he continued, 'must come in less than five years if major violence is to be avoided.'

Between these two views lies the issue whether the principle of majority rule is being infringed upon or whether it is somehow being promoted within the colony. The British prime minister actually argues, by implication, both ways. At present, he recognises, the principle is infringed upon in practice. But, as the constitution contains a built-in measure of evolution towards the principle, the latter – through the constitution – finds the means of its rectification and is therefore being promoted. This is what the prime minister appears to have intended in appending to the above statement the following: 'It is really a question of pace.' In short, all good things come to pass in time. The difficulty with this view is that it ignores the tenuous nature of a thirty-year promise and the impatience – and, indeed, the desperation – of the African majority forced on them by the deplorable conditions of their existence.

Such exclusion of Africans from the political process is, however, frequently excused by the widespread belief that the European population of Southern Rhodesia, like that of South Africa, has been established in the colony for generations, and that the enfranchisement of Africans would create a grave risk of the subsequent expulsion of Europeans from their own country of origin. Apart from the objection that skilled expatriate labour (for the most part, almost invariably and inescapably European) will be necessary for the development of the country for an appreciable time to come, there is another fact to consider. This is that the European population is actually composed in the main of individuals who left their countries at a mature age to take advantage of the substantial privileges and opportunities accorded to them under Southern Rhodesian law.

Southern Rhodesia, in company with Northern Rhodesia and Nyasaland, formed from 1953 to 1963 the Central African Federation. Full statistics on Southern Rhodesia's Europeans are difficult to obtain for that period, since they were compiled on a federal basis. But Mr Colin Leys,* in 1959, argued that on the basis of available evidence, it was likely that native born Rhodesians formed a minority of the European electorate. In fact, only 39 per cent of all Europeans living in the Federation were born there: 25 per cent were born in South Africa, 24 per cent in the United Kingdom and 12 per cent elsewhere. From this and similar information, it becomes difficult to escape the conclusion that a large majority of Southern Rhodesia's present European electorate – and of adult 'Rhodesians' – were not born in the colony at all and are only Rhodesian through adoption.

* C. Leys, *European Politics in Southern Rhodesia*, Oxford University Press 1959, p. 74.

When the federation was formed in 1953, political control of its government was given to the European voters. But in 1960, following violent opposition to the federation in Nyasaland, a new constitution was promulgated for that territory, with the consequent enfranchisement of 100,000 of the 2,900,000 African inhabitants there. With power decisively transferred to Africans, the new Nyasaland Legislative Assembly rejected the maintenance of the federal union. Similar protests among Africans in Northern Rhodesia produced similar results, and so the Legislative Assembly of that territory opposed, in its turn, the survival of the federation.

In 1957, Mr Garfield Todd, then prime minister of Southern Rhodesia, attempted in anticipation of similar events to broaden the franchise while preserving European supremacy. He failed and was later forced to resign. The new prime minister, Sir Edgar Whitehead, negotiated a new constitution with Britain in 1961. It featured the removal of safeguards for African interests and the introduction of a new electoral system. An election under this new system in December of 1962 brought to power the Rhodesian Front Party which advocated a policy of vigorous apartheid and the break-up of the federation.

Thus, with the legislatures of all three territories now opposed to the Union, it had to be, and was, brought to an end – on December 31st, 1963. But what was left in Southern Rhodesia was not a government representative of majority interests or views. What was left was a minority settler regime dedicated to the exclusion of African participation in government. Northern Rhodesia and Nyasaland objected to the federal union because they saw in it an instrument of settler domination. The Legislature of Southern Rhodesia rejected the union as well, since it now came to imply the subverting of settler domination.

The government of Southern Rhodesia is elected by less than 6 per cent of the population. All constitutional means of protest or reform have been denied to over 94 per cent of the population on the basis of race. ZAPU (The Zimbabwe African People's Union) and ZANU (The Zimbabwe African National Union) which are supported by the overwhelming majority of the population cannot operate freely. In fact, ZAPU has been proscribed. The leaders of both parties have been severely harassed by the settler government and banished to remote areas. Virtually all political activity by Africans has been declared illegal. Almost anything the African says or does in his own defence makes him liable to imprisonment for sedition. The political process, therefore, excludes and victimizes the African.

Nevertheless, an attempt is made to suggest that Southern Rhodesia's Africans are not excluded. Membership of the colonial legislature, in 1962, was enlarged to 65 seats. It must be remembered that Europeans constitute 5·7 per cent of the population and Africans 93·9 per cent. Nevertheless, of these seats 50 were allotted to Europeans and 15 to Africans. This is to say that one-twentieth of the population control 80 per cent of legislative representation. As the constitution may be amended by the vote of any 44 members, and as European members are in general agreement regarding the depressed status of Africans, the 15 seats granted the latter must be looked upon as window dressing intended, primarily, to impress the British public.

However, even the seats 'allotted' to Africans cannot actually be controlled by the Africans. For, in Southern Rhodesia, there is a dual system of electoral rolls. The 'A' Roll, which returns 50 legislators, comprises 91,000 electors, only 2,562 of whom are Africans. The 'B' Roll, which returns 15 legislators, comprises 11,197 electors, 681 of whom are Europeans. But due to provisions for cross voting, electors on one roll may also vote for candidates intended to be elected by the other. A system of weighting assigns the relative values of votes. The net result is that 50 Europeans *must* be elected, while the 15 African candidates – not all of whom are African – must usually be favoured by European electors in order to be chosen. Thus, the colony's constitution ensures that African voters in 50 constituencies will be restricted to about 3 per cent of the total electorate. It also ensures that European electors will largely determine which African candidates are chosen in the remaining 15 districts.

Some people in Britain take the view that, in time, at a gradual pace the situation will so evolve that power is peacefully transferred to the African majority.* But, in contrast to this hope, certain facts must be faced. First the present electoral system mathematically ensures, through various complicated procedures, that the 'A' Roll vote must never count for less than 80 per cent of the total vote – no matter how many 'A' or 'B' Roll voters cast their ballots. Second, salary, property and education requirements for 'A' Roll voter registration are such that the upper limit has almost been reached for Africans who might qualify to register; and the number of these, on a generous, outside estimate is 5,000. Third, European 'A' Roll voters increased by 9,116 within one year (1961–1962) and presently represent 94·7 per cent all voters on this roll. Thus, there is no empirical basis for the sanguine hopes expressed by many, including the present British prime minister, in regard to a gradual and peaceful transfer of power to the majority. The electoral system is so rigged that impoverished Africans could never come to within hailing distance of the electoral defeat of wealthy Europeans.

Even were it conceivable that within 30 years this might be done, there is no assurance that the European electorate, which in fact controls the amendment procedures, would permit it. All the evidence, actually, points in the contrary direction. Increasingly, the settler electorate of Southern Rhodesia has opposed all liberalising trends. Europeans in office who have advocated an easing of restrictions placed upon African political participation have been removed.

Mr Garfield Todd, the liberal prime minister who declared for the lifting of the colour bar and who then also called for the addition of six to ten thousand Africans to the voters' roll, was swiftly driven out of office. One writer† suggests that the Todd case affords 'almost medical insight ... into the Rhodesian mind. In forty years of settler politics, only one prime minister has been scuttled in office, and this accolade was accorded to the one reformer in power that the system ever produced. Garfield Todd ... was a New Zealander ... In broad terms, his mistake

* The settler prime minister, Mr Ian Smith, said that he did not expect Africans in Southern Rhodesia to exercise such power within his lifetime.
† Kheatley, op. cit., p. 249.

was to break the infallible rule for success in Rhodesian politics – "Keep Right"'.

Even Sir Edgar Whitehead, the new prime minister, proved insufficiently conservative. He fell. The same fate, in April 1964, overtook Mr Winston Field, who was thought by the right-wing to be too ineffective in regard to the wresting of independence from Britain. The mantle of leadership settled about the shoulders of Mr Ian Smith, the present prime minister, who, under Mr Field's regime, made outright references to the benefits of a unilateral declaration of independence from Britain and who recently (June 6th, 1964) told a crowd that even a 'thread of an apron string' linking Southern Rhodesia to Britain was unacceptable.

It seems beyond question that the attitude, prejudices and economic interests of the European electorate in Southern Rhodesia require that their electoral intentions towards Africans be viewed from a severely realistic, which is to say doubtful, perspective. One may reasonably suppose that the granting of independence to Southern Rhodesia would be disastrous in at least one of the two respects mentioned above. Britain has granted independence to minority regimes only twice in her history as an imperial power. South Africa was the first in 1910. Zanzibar was the second in December of 1963. As for the first, despite entrenched clauses in the constitution protecting the rights of Africans, these were swept away following independence by the European minority. In regard to the second, namely Zanzibar, an anti-British revolution destroyed the newly established government within 34 days of its birth. In either case, these ensuing developments could have been avoided by establishing fully representative governments before independence was declared.

The fact that Southern Rhodesia is on the Agenda of the UN and has been the subject of discussion at the Security Council and at the Committee of Twenty-four on Decolonisation, has reinforced the view that the question of Southern Rhodesia is a threat to peace in the area concerned. This is so not only because of the massive armed forces acquired by Southern

SETTLER POLITICS

Rhodesia, but its challenge to the principle 'one man, one vote'; its determination to perpetuate a European settler government, and its links with apartheid South Africa, the Katanga lobby, and the Portuguese territories in Africa, forming the 'Unholy Alliance'. For all these reasons, moral, legal, historical, and also because Southern Rhodesia has international implications, Britain has a responsibility to ensure that Mr Ian Smith does not declare unilateral independence. If this is declared, then it is the duty of Britain to take punitive measures which she is legally and morally entitled to do because Southern Rhodesia is still her colony.

A point which must now be established is that Southern Rhodesia is still a colony, and not an independent state. She is a British colony and the United Kingdom has sovereign authority over her. When a British colony acquires independence, British authority is relinquished. But, until accession to independence is achieved, the United Kingdom's responsibility for that colony, *vis-à-vis* other states and international organisations is retained. This legal position cannot be obliterated by Britain's oft-repeated references to conventional privileges 'enjoyed' by Southern Rhodesia over a period of years.

In October of 1962, the General Assembly of the United Nations requested by a majority of 81 to 2 (with 19 abstentions) that the United Kingdom secure for the people under its authority in Southern Rhodesia the right to vote. This body made similar requests on 14th October and 6th November of 1963. The African heads of state and government, convening in Addis Ababa in May of 1963, further requested that Britain not transfer to a foreign racial minority in the Colony the 'attributes of sovereignty'.

Far from making every effort to abort the growth of minority, racialist and unrepresentative government in Rhodesia, the British government made, on the contrary, substantial concessions to the latter, and of such a nature, as to make Rhodesia's power and policies all the more formidable and uncompromising. Foremost among these concessions was the transfer of powerful armed forces, including 18 Canberra bombers, 14

Vampire fighter-bombers and 13 Supersonic Hawker Hunter fighters, previously under British command, to the settler government of Southern Rhodesia at the time of the Federation's dissolution on 31st December, 1963.

In reply to United Nations appeals to the effect that fully representative government be established on a 'one man one vote' basis, the British government has argued that a parliamentary convention prevents it exercising to the full its legal authority over Southern Rhodesia. The convention is said to derive from the fact that for 40 years successive British governments did not use their powers to safeguard the interests of the African inhabitants, and that, in effect, these powers became obsolete. The bare bones of this idea is that, because Britain *has not* interfered with the internal machinery of Southern Rhodesia's government, it therefore *cannot* do so *in law*. This contention has no juridical justification.

For the first thirty years of its colonial history, Southern Rhodesia was ruled by the British South Africa Company, a private trading concern. This company was nevertheless subject to the over-riding control of the British government, which had granted the concern a royal charter setting out the broad lines of governmental policy. The company was established to prospect for gold, and as there was little of it, proceeded to sell to European settlers, at profit, farmland which had been wrested from Africans. It was to satisfy these settlers that the company set up a Legislative Council over which they, the settlers ultimately acquired control. Finally, during the First World War, the company surrendered its rights of administering the Protectorate in exchange for compensation paid by Britain and the settler government.

The small group of Europeans then living in Rhodesia were offered the choice either of affiliating the colony with South Africa or of becoming self-governing. They opted for the latter by a vote of 8,774 to 5,989. This referendum, which occurred in 1923, did not, of course, reflect the wishes, interests or participation of an African populace which, by contrast with the European, was numerically vast. Nevertheless, British representatives at the United Nations have argued that this referendum constituted the prime democratic event of Southern Rhodesia history, legitimately determining the future of British non-interference and withdrawal. Still, despite these histrionics, and despite the granting of self-government to the settlers, the British government imposed by law the same control over their activities as it had over the activities of the company. Further to this, the notion that Southern Rhodesia had enjoyed control of its own internal affairs for forty years is false. For the United Kingdom appointed the Governor whose official instructions gave him express and lawful authority to refuse to accept the advice of his colonial ministers.

A convention, legally, is one only if it is recognised as such. If its recognition is essentially unilateral in a given case, that recognition may be unilaterally withdrawn without prejudice to the law. The history of the recognition of the Southern Rhodesia convention only goes back to 1957. It is contained in a joint announcement of the United Kingdom Government and the Federation of Rhodesia and Nyasaland and does not actually refer to Southern Rhodesia as a separate political entity. The substance of the announcement reads to the effect that 'The United Kingdom recognises the existence of a convention ... whereby the United Kingdom in practice does not initiate any legislation to amend or to repeal any Federal Act or to deal with any matter included within the competence of the Federal Legislature except at the request of the Federal Government.' Subsequently, the Southern Rhodesian government besought of the United Kingdom some such similar *recognition* in its own regard; and this would constitute little other than a plea that the United Kingdom undertake, unilaterally in respect of Southern Rhodesia, to follow a policy of domestic non-interference. The British government at no time introduced legislation to this effect. But in June, 1961, a British White Paper, relating to constitutional proposals for Southern Rhodesia, declared that such a convention as spoken of above did exist.

What was essentially involved, however, was not the 'recognition' but the *creation* of a convention. Such recognition, in short, rested upon little other than the creation of a policy, a political policy, primarily intended to extricate the British government from its responsibilities in Southern Rhodesia. This policy, in effect, required that the United Kingdom treat Southern Rhodesia as a fully sovereign government except in so far as this government *agreed* to any United Kingdom legislation which was sought to be enacted in its regard. What happened, therefore, was that the United Kingdom, in law fully sovereign over Southern Rhodesia, would in practice abdicate from sovereignty on the principle that in practice it had already abdicated.

However the British Attorney-General, Sir John Hobson, in reply to questions during a Parliamentary debate on 16th July, 1963, stated that it was not quite accurate to say 'that the convention had existed for 40 years'. He argued instead that it had 'coalesced or congealed into the formality of a convention much more recently'... so recently in fact as 1961. Finally, in regard to British parliamentary authority over Southern Rhodesia, he suggested that 'the convention and its relevance to the powers of this Parliament and whether they should be exercised may be subject to discussion hereafter'.

In this last statement the Attorney-General is, in effect, asserting that the Southern Rhodesia convention is actually subject, even now, to Parliamentary review. Thus, it highlights a basic contradiction in the entire British position. For, either the convention establishes the juridical independence of Southern Rhodesia, which can be infringed only on its express agreement, and thus, in that event, not 'infringed' at all; or the convention merely attests to an internal redistribution of authority under a sovereign power, there being no irreversible derogation of control, such that parliamentary review of the convention is always juridically in order. But it becomes in any event impossible to argue that in practice Rhodesia is independent, while arguing, too, that more ultimately she is not. But of course she is not.

The Monckton Commission (including the Chief Justice of Southern Rhodesia and the Attorney-General of the Federation) which was appointed by the British Government in July of 1959* was in unanimous agreement that the Federation, and consequently Southern Rhodesia, 'falls short of the status of a

* Report published in October, 1960 (Cmnd. 1148).

full international person', that 'it is not an independent sovereign state', and that 'it is the United Kingdom who remain ultimately responsible in international law'. The Commissioners found, further, that 'the United Kingdom Parliament has inherent power to legislate for any part of Her Majesty's dominions except in so far as this has been qualified by the Statute of Westminster' and in regard to Southern Rhodesia there was and is no such qualification. As affecting the joint announcement of 1957 the Commissioners categorically stated that it referred 'only to powers conferred upon the Federal Legislature' without affecting 'the legislative authority of the United Kingdom Parliament to provide for the future constitutional development of the Federation, and, for this purpose, to make any necessary amendments to the Constitution itself'. The Monckton Commission, therefore, set up by the British Government to review the constitutional position in the Federation, clearly took the view that British sovereignty remained, even so far as to entail the right to amend the Southern Rhodesian Constitution, and, indeed that it was and 'is essential that this right *should* be retained'.

If the interpretation of parliamentary conventions as laid down by the Monckton Commission is correct, then even if such a convention did exist in regard to Southern Rhodesia it could not diminish parliament's right to legislate for the colony without reference to the colonial government. And even though the British parliament has not for the last 40 years exercised its undoubted right to legislate for Southern Rhodesia without the agreement of its government, all British constitutional authorities are agreed that it is not in this manner that parliamentary conventions are established. In fact, many examples are to be found in British constitutional history of a parliament legislating without the consent of the government of a self-governing colony in order to correct colonial injustices or to set aside a colonial constitution unsuitable for the conditions of its time.

In this respect, the Maltese and Southern Rhodesian constitutions were enacted by Britain by the same process shortly after each other – in 1921 and 1923 respectively. All leading British constitutional authorities (e.g. Sir Arthur Barriedale Keith,

Minty and Lord Hailsham) regarded them for all practical purposes as identical. Yet, in 1936, the British parliament revoked the Maltese constitution without regard to 'Conventions'.

In conclusion, Britain's legal authority over Southern Rhodesia remains intact. And that authority imposes the need to accept certain responsibilities. One of the most basic of Britain's responsibilities must be to establish secure conditions for representative government in the colony. And government cannot be truly representative if political expression and power are denied to a majority on grounds of race. European settlers have an undoubted stake in the future of Southern Rhodesia. The stake of the African majority, however, cannot reasonably be conceived as less than theirs. There is no *necessary* conflict of interests between these communities. In so far as serious conflict, overt and latent, exists, it is essentially attributable to the present political and economic structure of racial favouritism. Kenya's example of racial peace and co-operation since independence points the way forward. The basis for progress does not lie in minority rule. And, ultimately, the security of the European community cannot be built upon it. If this community cannot or chooses not to understand, there is no legal or moral reason for the government of the United Kingdom to accede to its folly. Britain can act. She must act. She has the right and, therefore, the duty.

3

SOUTHERN RHODESIA: 'PARTICULAR AND URGENT ISSUES'

The central African Federation lasted for only ten years. The decision to bring it to an end was taken at the Central African Conference held at Victoria Falls in July 1963. During the following year, Zambia and Malawi successfully negotiated with the British government for full independence. But the break-up of the CAF affected Southern Rhodesia in a different way since the country had been internally self-governed for forty years under white minority rule.

When the 1961 Southern Rhodesian constitution replaced that of 1923, the autonomy of the government was widened to eliminate much of the British government's reserved power in regard to African interests and constitutional amendments. This reserved power was replaced by the addition of a Declaration of Rights and a constitutional council both of which were said to be designed to protect the legitimate interests of all the people of Southern Rhodesia. As a result of these changes, the only effective power left in the hands of the British government was the power to grant or withhold full independence.

A major issue affecting the position of the African majority in Southern Rhodesia on the break-up of the CAF was the question of the armed forces. Previously, these had been under British command, and this had to some extent been a safeguard for the African majority. But when in July 1963 it was decided to end the CAF it became apparent that it was Britain's intention to hand over command of Southern Rhodesia's armed forces to the settler government. This would have the effect of greatly *strengthening the settler government and of making it even more difficult for the African people of Southern Rhodesia to obtain majority rule. Control of the armed forces, and particularly the air force, would give the settler government the means to suppress any nationalist risings and possibly to keep the African people in permanent subjection.*

In an attempt to prevent Britain from handing over command of the armed forces to the settlers, Nkrumah initiated an appeal for a meeting of the UN Security Council to consider the whole question of Southern Rhodesia. The request was made in a letter dated 2 August 1963 from the UN delegations of Ghana, Guinea, Morocco and Egypt. At the same time, the Ghana government 'Memorandum in regard to Southern Rhodesia' quoted in Chapter 2, was submitted to the President of the Security Council. Copies of the Memorandum were given to all members of the Security Council on 21 August under cover of a note verbale. The Ghanaian delegation formally requested its circulation as a Security Council document on 28 August, and it was distributed as UN document S/5403.

With the gaining of independence of the African colonial territories of Britain, France and Belgium, African membership of the UN had increased rapidly from 1957, the year of Ghana's independence. Largely due to Nkrumah's efforts there had begun to develop an 'African lobby' at the UN. Before important debates of vital concern to Africa, members of African delegations would meet and if possible agree on a common line. There was no difficulty in getting united support for resolutions in favour of African people still subjected to colonialism, or the rule of settler, minority governments. But as Nkrumah pointed out: 'It is an illusion to suppose because Africa as a whole can cast thirty-six votes in the General Assembly of the United Nations this makes us powerful. Even when we have voted as a united group on such issues as South Africa and Southern Rhodesia, what has it availed us? In practice – nothing. . . . Pious resolutions are no substitute for positive action.'* Nkrumah saw that a single African vote in the UN would be more effective than the votes of any number of separate African states, if that vote represented the voice of the African people expressed through a Union Government of Africa.

The speech of the Ghanaian delegate in the UN Security Council was made in September 1963. He spoke on behalf of all the independent states of Africa 'seeking to effect the complete eradication of colonialism . . . and

---

* Address in the National Assembly, Accra, 3 September 1965.

SOUTHERN RHODESIA

to put an end to the inhuman and undemocratic white minority rule in Africa'. But as Nkrumah foresaw, the efforts of the African lobby failed to prevent the transfer by Britain of Southern Rhodesia's armed forces to the settler government. The resolution put by Ghana was supported in the Security Council not only by the African members, Ghana and Morocco, but by all the other non-permanent members. Britain was the only member of the Council opposed to it, and Britain used its veto to prevent it being passed. As a result, the armed forces of Southern Rhodesia were handed over to the settler government on 31 December 1963 when the CAF was officially ended.

Extracts from the Ghanaian delegate's speech in the United Nation Security Council, 9 September 1963

The delegations of Ghana, Guinea, Morocco and the United Arab Republic, in a letter dated 2 August 1963 [S/5382], together with an explanatory memorandum addressed to the President of the Security Council, requested a meeting of the Council to be convened in accordance with rule 2 of the provisional rules of procedure of the Security Council for the purpose of examining the question of Southern Rhodesia in the light of recent developments in that territory. As I have said, this request is unanimously supported by the other twenty-eight African delegations whose decision was communicated to the President of the Security Council by the Chairman of the African group of Member states, the Charge d'Affaires of Congo (Brazzaville), in a letter dated 30 August 1963 [S/5409]. This unanimous approach of the African States has demonstrated once more that in the anti-colonial struggle, Africa speaks with one clear unmistakable voice.

But my delegation must make it clear from the very outset that no African state takes delight in coming to the Security Council. When we request a meeting of the Council, it must be on a grave and urgent issue. Therefore, while the request before the Council must be viewed as part of the systematic process by which all the independent African states are seeking to effect complete eradication of colonialism from their continent and to put an end to the inhuman and undemocratic white minority rule in Africa, the question of Southern Rhodesia raises particular and urgent issues which, on the information at present available, appear to all African states to constitute a serious threat to the peace and security of the African continent.

Within a very short space of time, possibly within weeks, there will be transferred to the exclusive control of the Southern Rhodesian government, the most powerful air force at present existing on the African continent, together with a small but highly efficient army recruited on a racial basis. My government has obtained detailed reports on the air force. It is more powerful even than the South African Air Force at the moment and is stronger than the metropolitan and colonial air forces of Portugal put together. In order to avoid any dispute as to these facts, my government has had a study made by a leading British firm of aircraft consultants which, if I have your permission, Mr President, I will pass on to members of the Council.

Broadly speaking, the air force which will be shortly transferred to Southern Rhodesia consists of two modern fighter-bomber squadrons which could be used either against the civil population or for offensive purposes outside the territory, and two bomber squadrons which are only designed for use outside Southern Rhodesia and supporting aircraft including long-distance troop carriers. It must be realised that in Southern Rhodesia the African population is particularly susceptible to indiscriminate air attack. Out of a total African population of around 3,700,000, well over 2 million are peasants living in segregated farming lands where Europeans are not permitted to reside. Close on 700,000 more live in what that distinguished United States scholar, and my friend, Professor Thomas Franck, has called 'the African ghettos', which are far from European townships. It is therefore possible to make indiscriminate attacks on the great bulk of the African population without even running the risk of injuring any European. As will be seen from the technical report which I have passed around, the aircraft being transferred can be used to drop incendiary material like napalm, and are normally equipped with rockets and other air-to-ground missiles. None of these weapons could of course be used for the

SOUTHERN RHODESIA

purpose of controlling a riot or other civil disturbances. They are essentially weapons of mass terrorism.

The ratio of training aircraft to fighters and bombers further suggests that the air force to be taken over has been designed for rapid expansion. One of the arguments which has been made – and in fact just repeated by the representative of the United Kingdom – against the Security Council considering the question of Southern Rhodesia is that everything is calm and quiet in that territory at the moment. But then it can also be argued that if this is in fact so, it is very difficult to see why the Southern Rhodesian white minority government requires these aircraft so urgently. It may of course be that the Southern Rhodesian government does not require this force primarily for action inside 'our territory' – which they call their territory – but for aggressive action against neighbouring states. Indeed, how can a contrary view be held in view of Winston Field's pronouncements? In fact, the possibility of hostile action is suggested by the technical information, which members have before them, one passage of which I shall quote as an illustration:

'For attack the Rhodesian Air Force has 18 Canberra B4s. These are the heaviest combat jet aircraft in Africa apart from Tupolev Tu-16 Badger aircraft operated by the United Arab Republic. Unlike the Canberra force in, for instance, Peru, numbering less than one squadron, the two squadrons in Rhodesia constitute a big enough force to be militarily viable. The Canberra was designed to take the standard British and American atomic weapons which are currently several times more powerful than the bombs that destroyed the Japanese cities in World War II. The Canberra is well suited to carry air-to-ground missiles, specially the Bullpup, either atomic or non-atomic, and the Nord AS-30.

'With wing-tip extra fuel, underwing rockets, bombs, napalm, and with bombs or fuel in the bomb bay, the Canberra remains one of the world's formidable weapons.'

I should like to quote one sentence from the Consultants' conclusions, which reads as follows:

'They are therefore able to inflict severe punishment at short notice and present a situation to which neighbours have necessarily had to adjust themselves.'

Without wishing to revive former bitter feelings, my delegation must point out that seven years ago the United Arab Republic was engaged in a military conflict with two major powers, yet the long-range bomber strength of the United Arab Republic air force is nothing in comparison in numbers with the long-range bomber strength of the air force it is proposed to transfer to Southern Rhodesia.

Up till now this powerful air force has been under the control of the so-called Central African Federation, which meant in practice that it was under British control. So long as it was under British control, this was to us a redeeming feature. But to have it transferred to the white minority government presents a grave crisis. If one turns to the official United Kingdom reports of the period, it is clear, for example, that the British government was able to deploy the then Federal Air Force in Cyprus and in the Aden Protectorate, and indeed certain of the aircraft are specially equipped for fighting in the Near East. Now, it is this gigantic and powerful air force which is going to be placed at the disposal of the white minority government of Southern Rhodesia. Is my colleague from the United Kingdom in a position to tell the Council why such a force is being transferred and, further, is he in a position to tell the Council what reasons, if any, the Southern Rhodesian Government gave for wishing to have this air force transferred to it?

I am sure that the representative of the United Kingdom will realise the importance of the answer to these questions. If it was because the internal political situation is now so critical that the British and Southern Rhodesian governments both believed that the settler government could only maintain its position by threatening the African inhabitants with mass destruction by napalm bombs – and rockets, then clearly the situation is one which the Security Council should investigate at once. The use of napalm bombs in Angola is still so fresh in our memories as to cause grave concern at the possible extension of their use in

Africa by much more powerful aircraft. If, on the other hand, the British government were assured by the Southern Rhodesian government that the internal situation was calm at home, then for what purpose did the Southern Rhodesian government require this air force?

I must say that, from our own independent inquiries, the maintenance of this air force is beyond the resources of Southern Rhodesia. The same thing has been said by even Sir Roy Welensky. Even the government of Southern Rhodesia as at present constituted could not undertake responsibility for such forces if, in the first place, it did not intend to use them, or, secondly, if it was not fairly sure of recouping to some extent the very high costs involved. I will therefore ask another question. Has the representative of the United Kingdom any knowledge of an arrangement with any power – and in this I include the United Kingdom – to bear the whole or a part of the cost of this force?

Again, I am sure that the representative of the United Kingdom will realise the importance of this question. If any power on the African continent or outside it has promised to subsidize, either directly or indirectly, by paying for other services which the Southern Rhodesian government cannot otherwise meet owing to its heavy new armament commitment, then whatever power has made such an agreement is not only directly subsidizing repression of the African population in Southern Rhodesia but is also starting an arms race on the African continent, thus endangering the peace and security of that continent. Obviously, no African state within range of the Southern Rhodesian Air Force – and these include the Commonwealth countries and, of course, Northern Rhodesia and Nyasaland – could idly look on without some counter-armament.

The United Kingdom Minister responsible for Central Africa, Mr R. A. Butler, has stated that there are no secret agreements with Britain, and I of course accept that. Nevertheless, in view of the circumstantial stories appearing in the British press to the contrary, it might be desirable for the representative of the United Kingdom to give the Council some further specific assurance. The real issue, however, is whether there is a secret agreement between Southern Rhodesia, Portugal, and South Africa, by which these powers would pay for the cost of the Air Force. In this connection, may I quote a paragraph from the *Observer* of London of March 1963. The correspondent of the *Observer*, writing from Salisbury, said:

> 'Sir Roy has recently raised the salaries of top Army and Air Force officers. About £9 million is now being spent annually on "defence" in the Federation, and one question Sir Roy is continually asking is how the Federation's individual territories could bear such a burden in the event of a Federal dissolution.
>
> 'He has not said against whom an independent Nyasaland or Northern Rhodesia would need to defend itself.
>
> 'Great interest was aroused here recently when *Newscheck*, a South African news magazine, reported that Mr Winston Field, the Southern Rhodesian Prime Minister, who is on record as favouring a "Nato-type" defence alliance between Southern Rhodesia, Angola, Mozambique and South Africa, has been given definite promises of financial and military help without strings by the South African Government.'

It is unlikely, of course, that, if such an agreement were made, Mr Winston Field would tell the British government of it prior to the final transfer of the air force, but I would like the representative of the United Kingdom at least to consider whether it is not possible that such an agreement might in fact have been made, unknown to the United Kingdom government.

This brings me to yet another question which I hope the representative of the United Kingdom will be able to answer because it is germane to the whole issue now under discussion in the Security Council. On Thursday, 5 September 1963, after document S/5403 had been published, the London diplomatic correspondent of the *Guardian* reported this as the view of the United Kingdom government:

> 'Britain, in fact, will retain control over the external defence

of Southern Rhodesia, including the deployment of her forces outside Rhodesia and questions of defence agreements with other countries. Under such an arrangement there is no question of the forces being used, for instance, in the Congo. It was recalled that the Federal government had previously been restrained from action when events there could have been considered a threat to the Federation itself.'

But time and time again the United Nations have been told by the United Kingdom representatives that, quite apart from the technical legal position, the British government is powerless to deal with the Southern Rhodesian question in practice, whatever the legal position.

My question is therefore this: how is this control in practice going to be exercised by the government of the United Kingdom? I am sure that the members of the Council realise the importance of this question. There will be a Defence Minister responsible only to the Southern Rhodesian government. If then this minister decides, for example, to deploy the air force which is proposed to transfer to Southern Rhodesia, in Angola or Mozambique, how in practice can the British government stop this minister? How is it that the United Kingdom now finds that it has, after all, power at a moment's notice to revoke the deployment of the Southern Rhodesian Air Force outside Southern Rhodesian frontiers? If, in fact, the British government continues to have this authority over the Southern Rhodesian government, then how is it that it says that it is powerless to call a constitutional conference, as the United Nations has repeatedly requested? Let us be brutally frank here. In our opinion, the United Kingdom government has ultimate authority and power in Southern Rhodesia, and it must exercise these powers, however residual, in the name of African advancement and peace and not for settler entrenchment in Southern Rhodesia.

Now let me deal with the position of the Army. Once again, from the factual inquiries which the government of Ghana has made, the statement contained in paragraph 16 at the memorandum submitted to the Security Council in regard to the transfer of European troops appears to be an understatement.

The present position is that there is one all-white battalion of regular troops who are recruited mainly from Britain, though the officer class is drawn not only from British but also from South African officers. There is also in the course of formation a second regular battalion of all-white troops for which the officer class will come largely from Britain and South Africa and the men from the United Kingdom. In addition to these there are four white territorial battalions. The permanently employed officers and non-commissioned officers for these territorial battalions come mainly from Britain and South Africa, but the reservist component is drawn exclusively from the white settler class. These are given an initial four and a half months' full-time training and subsequently attend army centres for extensive further training during their period of service.

In 1960, when the Monckton Commission reported on conditions in the Federation,* a number of members of the Commission, including British members of parliament supporting the present British administration, pointed out in an annex to the report the grave dangers of the organisation of such a force, which never existed in Southern Rhodesia prior to the Federation in 1953. They pointed out that if the so-called Federal government's argument was correct that the African people were being terrorised by small groups of African extremists, then clearly the great bulk of the African people would have equal interests with the European settlers in maintaining law and order. In fine, this all-white army has two features. So far as the regular officers and men are concerned, it is almost entirely a mercenary force. So far as the non-permanent territorial component is concerned, it is drawn from a tiny minority of the white population who are determined to oppose by force any advance of human dignity, equality and justice in Southern Rhodesia. Need I point out the lesson of history which shows inevitably that either type of these forces leads ultimately to increasing repression and the most violent and bitter type of civil war. If our organisation took steps to eliminate mercenaries

* Report of the Advisory Commission on the Review of the Constitution of Rhodesia and Nyasaland, London, H.M. Stationery Office, Cmnd. 1148.

from Katanga as a threat to peace, is there not a duty on this highest organ to take the same steps as in the case of Katanga? In the case of the regular battalion of all-white troops and the permanent cadres of the territorial army, no reason can exist why they should not return to their homelands, except that obviously someone would have to pay them compensation. Apparently this solution was never considered by the United Kingdom government at the Victoria Falls Conference, whose handling of the defence issue in general appears to have been most obscure. The impression has somehow been created that this matter was also discussed at the conference. In fact, of course, this was not so. The conference appears merely to have been asked to endorse a decision previously arrived at outside the conference. Mr Butler, the British minister responsible for Central Africa, was most explicit on this before the British House of Commons. On 11 July 1963 he said:

'... one has only to be in Central Africa to realise the intense anxiety of everyone as to their own future and the future of their own country.

'I therefore summoned a meeting of heads of delegations, outside the conference aided by the Minister of Defence of the Federation ... and we reached an agreement which the Conference endorsed.'*

In fact, if one looks at the composition of this meeting 'held outside the Conference' at which Mr Butler said 'we reached an agreement', no single African was represented, and the head of the delegation of Northern Rhodesia appears to have been an official recently appointed from Britain. Nyasaland was only represented by a civil servant observer. I leave the Council to draw the relevant conclusions from these facts. It may be that the representative of the United Kingdom can throw some light on why this procedure was adopted. The Ghana government had hoped that the United Kingdom government would be able to supply information, about which it asked some time ago in regard to the countries of origin of the members of the armed

* Parliamentary Debates (Hansard), House of Commons, Official Report, London, H.M. Stationery Office, Fifth Series, vol. 680, Session 1962–63, col. 1432.

forces. If the information is available now, it would be useful to have it.

. . . . .

Can you wonder that all African states are extremely concerned about the handing over of such forces to the control of a government formed from a political party which my friend, Sir Patrick Dean, described at the 1120th plenary meeting of the General Assembly on 28 June 1962, as the 'extreme right-wing European Party'. It is further worrying that this extreme rightwing European Party headed by Winston Field never accepted even the 1961 Constitution, illiberal as it is. All these developments and events give African states cause for serious concern and anxiety. In fact, as recently as May 1963, the heads of African states and governments at their conference at Addis Ababa, expressed grave concern over the situation in Southern Rhodesia. They unanimously passed a resolution dealing with this matter, of which I will read you certain operative paragraphs germane to the peace aspect of the Council's deliberation:

'*The Conference* . . .
'*Invites*, further, the colonial powers, particularly the United Kingdom with regard to Southern Rhodesia, not to transfer the powers and attributes of sovereignty to foreign minority governments imposed on African peoples by the use of force and under cover of racial legislation; and the transfer of power to settler minorities would amount to a violation of the provision of United Nations Resolution 1514 (XV) on independence;
'*Reaffirms* its support of African nationalists of Southern Rhodesia and solemnly declares that if power in Southern Rhodesia were to be usurped by a racial white minority Government, State Members of the Conference' – that is, African States – 'would lend their effective moral and practical support to any legitimate measures which the African nationalist leaders may devise for the purpose of

recovering such power and restoring it to the African majority ...'

Members of the Council will note that the preoccupation of the heads of African States in Addis Ababa in May was that the United Kingdom government had already in contemplation at that time the transfer of all the real powers and attributes of sovereignty to Southern Rhodesia, while at the same time obscuring the position by withholding technical sovereignty. This was recognised even by Mr Winston Field and he said so himself in some of his correspondence with the United Kingdom government. He wrote to Mr Butler on 20 April 1963, pointing out:

> 'When the Federation does come to an end on the secession of either Northern Rhodesia or Nyasaland, the functions and powers formerly exercised by the Southern Rhodesian government before entry into Federation will revert to Southern Rhodesia in as full a degree as they existed before that time, and in fact, in a fuller degree, in so far as they will now be operated under the 1961 Constitution, whereby the United Kingdom government's reserve powers have been eliminated except for certain formal items.'

In our view the break-up of the Federation presented the United Kingdom with great opportunities for a solution to the problem we are now discussing. In fact, a solution was put forward by Mr Kenneth Kaunda of Northern Rhodesia and the Northern Rhodesian delegation at the Victoria Falls Conference. According to the United Kingdom White Paper dealing with the report of the Central African Conference, the Northern Rhodesian delegation put forward a proposal which would in fact have prevented any important powers being transferred to the Southern Rhodesian government until such time as it was reconstituted on a democratic basis. If this proposal had been accepted or even allowed to be discussed it might have prevented this meeting of the Council. Paragraph 7 of this White Paper, after referring to the proposals of the United Kingdom and the Southern Rhodesian delegations, goes on to say:

'... The Northern Rhodesian delegation indicated that their approach to the problem was different. They considered that the United Kingdom government should at an early date appoint a Commissioner to take over all the functions of the Federal government, and then to arrange for the progressive transfer of those functions to the territorial governments ... This view was not, however, accepted by any other delegation, on the grounds that the process of dissolution ought to be worked out between the governments in advance of some date at which time the dissolution could or should take place. It was also made clear by the Chairman' – that is to say, the British Minister in Charge of Central African Affairs – 'that the concept of appointing a Commissioner to inherit the functions of the Federal government formed no part of Her Majesty's government policy.'*

From this White Paper, it is unfortunately only too apparent that the United Kingdom government was not prepared even to take into consideration a solution which would have enabled it to bring pressure on the Southern Rhodesian government and which was supported by the only delegation present which could claim to be in any way representative of African opinion. It is important to point out that at this conference, Nyasaland was not represented at all, except by European officials who came as observers and that therefore the United Kingdom government rejected on this occasion the only view which could be said to be the voice of African political parties.

The urgency of this serious situation has been accentuated by the enactment of a law by the British parliament, the Rhodesia and Nyasaland Act, 1963, which permits the United Kingdom government by the formal process of enacting an Order-in Council subsequently to make the necessary detailed provisions for the break-up of the Federation and the transfer of its powers. In short, the United Kingdom government can in law transfer at any time from now on all the powers and attributes of sovereignty, about which the heads of states of Africa com-

* Report of the Central Africa Conference, 1963, London, H.M. Stationery Office, Cmnd. 2093.

plained to the Southern Rhodesian government, without even necessarily obtaining the consent of the British parliament. When this hand-over will actually take place it is more difficult to estimate. But it is likely to be fairly soon.

The position is that the process of handing over of what are in fact the powers and attributes of sovereignty to Southern Rhodesia must at the very latest be completed by 31 December 1963. But the United Kingdom government has pledged itself to seek retrospective parliamentary approval of such powers that are in fact transferred before October 1963 and prior parliamentary approval of any powers transferred after that date. It would appear, however, that pressure of parliamentary business is likely to force the British government to seek approval of the transfer of all major powers within a week or so of the conclusion of the coming general debate at the eighteenth session of the General Assembly. This is why the Security Council must take preventive action, if future conflict is to be avoided.

It will be argued that the armed forces and the air force about which we are complaining are already *in situ* in Southern Rhodesia. But, as we have made it abundantly clear, the issue at stake is who controls them. With the dissolution of the so-called Central African Federation, the oppressive 'extreme right-wing European Party' wishes to gain control of these forces under a cloak of secrecy for reasons which are not far to seek. All African states, therefore, call upon the Council to consider the seriousness of this eventuality. Already, all members of the United Nations are aware of the organised oppression of the African population by the small European minority. The records of the United Nations are replete with the oppressive and repressive laws which have the actual force of the policy of apartheid.

The outcry of the African states against the undemocratic constitution of Southern Rhodesia is by no means confined to the African continent. . . . As long ago as 1955 the distinguished United States author, Mr John Gunther said:

'There are, no doubt, honest English people who have a

sentimental attachment to Rhodesia, and for that matter honest Rhodesians who have no basis of comparison with other countries and who are blind to what is happening under their noses, ignorant of the fact that racial discriminations in Rhodesia are among the most barbarous, shameful and disgusting in the world.'*

And this was at a time when perhaps the most liberal of the Southern Rhodesian Prime Ministers, Mr Garfield Todd, was in office.

If the Council would prefer authority from a quite different source, here is a statement issued by the Roman Catholic hierarchy in 1961, and signed by the Archbishop of Salisbury and the Bishops of Gwelo, Bulawayo and Umtali. With your permission, I quote the hierarchy's actual words:

> 'Wages are inadequate, housing conditions in many instances are unworthy of human beings, and terms of employment are such that husbands are separated for long periods from their wives. Such a state of affairs cries to heaven for vengeance and even in the natural order can only breed crime and chaos. Need we wonder if men are incited to subversive activity when there is such obvious disparity in the quantity and quality of land occupied by the two major racial groups in the country.'

I need not reiterate here the conviction which my delegation has long held, namely, the responsibility of the United Kingdom for the present state of affairs in Southern Rhodesia. The African states have never entertained any doubts about the conclusion of the Special Committee set up as a result of resolution 1745 (XVI) on the status of Southern Rhodesia. The Special Committee had stated unequivocally in its report,† 'that the territory of Southern Rhodesia is a Non-Self-Governing Territory in the meaning of Chapter XI of the Charter'. This has since been endorsed by the General Assembly and this

---

* *Inside Africa*, New York, Harper and Brothers, 1955, p. 632.
† Official Records of the General Assembly, Sixteenth Session, Annexes, agenda item 97, document A/5124, annex III.

view has been confirmed in subsequent General Assembly resolutions, particularly resolution 1760 (XVII) of 31 October 1962, which reaffirmed resolution 1747 (XVI) on 28 June 1962. The Special Committee in its resolution of 20 June 1963, also confirmed this conclusion.

It is a curious irony of fate that it was the United Kingdom which, according to Mr Wilfred Benson, who was present throughout the San Francisco Conference as an official, 'established a claim to the paternity of Chapter XI of our Charter by presenting principles of general policy'. Indeed, the view has long been widely held that the preservation of international peace and colonial emancipation are but two aspects of the same problem, and that therefore they are the direct concern of all Members of the United Nations. The late Mr John Foster Dulles said that Chapter XI of the Charter 'is not merely the concern of the colonial powers, but also the concern of the United Nations'. On this issue every African state would support the former Secretary of State of the United States. Why this is so has been explained by a distinguished Brazilian diplomat and lawyer, some of whose words on the matter, with your permission, I shall quote:

> 'From the point of view of originality and innovation, it is indisputable that the Declaration regarding non-self-governing territories stands out as one of the boldest and most positive contributions of the San Francisco Conference to the legal order of international relations. Nor can it be easily denied that Articles 73 and 74 are, amongst all the provisions of the Charter, those which most markedly bear the imprint of the political and juridical philosophy inherent in the system of the United Nations, as they assert the competence of that organisation to deal systematically with a whole set of social problems which hitherto had escaped comprehensive international control... The juridical expression of the ideal of universality ... would have been grossly distorted if the interests and aspirations of hundreds of millions in non-self-governing territories were to be left outside the law of the United Nations and under the exclusive competence of the

internal public law of the States holding jurisdiction over them.'

In 1923, the same year in which the British government enacted the Southern Rhodesian constitution and allowed a small minority of white settlers to enter into a plebiscite regardless of African aspirations, they set out in a White Paper their considered views on the relationship between Africans and settlers in Africa. This is generally known as the Devonshire Declaration, from the Duke of Devonshire, the then British Colonial Secretary. This Declaration states:

> '... His Majesty's Government think it is necessary definitely to record their considered opinion that the interest of the African natives must be paramount; and if, and when, those interests and the interests of the immigrant races should conflict the former should prevail.'*

We are asking the Council to bear this in mind.

Despite the fact that the resolution of the General Assembly of 14 December 1960, the famous resolution 1514 (XV), repeated in other words the Devonshire Declaration, so far as Southern Rhodesia is concerned, the United Kingdom has taken no effective steps to comply with this resolution, though they have complied with it in regard to other African territories under their control. Members of the Council will be familiar with operative paragraph 5 of this resolution, and it does no harm to repeat it here:

> 'Immediate steps shall be taken, in Trust and Non-Self-Governing Territories or all other territories which have not yet attained independence, to transfer all powers to the peoples of those territories, without any conditions or reservations, in accordance with their freely expressed will and desire, without any distinction as to race, creed or colour, in order to enable them to enjoy complete independence and freedom.'

I do not propose to say anything much at this stage about the supposed British Convention, though it would be interesting if

---

* *Indians in Kenya*, London, H.M. Stationery Office, Cmnd. 1922, p. 9.

the representative of the United Kingdom were able to tell the Council whether their alleged Convention has been in existence for forty years, a position which he has, as spokesman for the United Kingdom government, always maintained, or whether it has been in existence for only two years, which is what the British Attorney General recently told the House of Commons. However, I think I should point out that even in the British parliament there are grave doubts as to the existence of the convention.

Speaking on 11 July 1963 on the Rhodesia and Nyasaland Bill, the Opposition spokesman, Mr Bottomley, emphasised the power of the United Kingdom parliament to deal with the situation in Southern Rhodesia. He said:

'Let me say one thing further which I think the Government may have to consider ... That is that if the present Administration of Southern Rhodesia are not prepared in their own interests to advance at a rate which will give all sections of the community equality and a chance of practising democracy, we are left with one other weapon – we still have the power to suspend the Constitution and to withhold economic assistance.'*

Clearly, therefore, the Opposition spokesman did not recognise the existence of any such convention which, as they say, has been in existence for forty years. I was always taught that British parliamentary Conventions could only be held to exist if they were accepted at least by the two major parties in Parliament. If I am wrong about this, I stand to be corrected.

My delegation has produced the full facts both in our documents and in my present statement – full facts in regard to the inevitable revolutionary and explosive situation in Southern Rhodesia. We have demonstrated that the forces about to be transferred are far too big to be handed over to any colonial territory, let alone a white minority government representative

* Parliamentary Debates (Hansard), House of Commons, Official Report, Fifth Series, Vol. 681, Session 1962–63, London, H.M. Stationery Office, cols. 1450 and 1451.

of only 6 per cent of the European population and totally unrepresentative of the 94 per cent African population. We have demonstrated that, prior to the constitution of the Federation in 1953 no such forces and – as Mr Winston Field has pointed out – no such powers, in many instances, existed under the uncontrolled authority of the Southern Rhodesia government. In fact, it can be said that this is the first time in history that Britain has planned to hand over large armed forces and certain other powers to a government over which it has repeatedly stated within these Council chambers that it has no control.

From these facts it must be clear to every member of the Council that the transfer of the armed forces and powerful air force to Southern Rhodesia cannot but result in a conflict on the African continent. This is why we have come here to ask for an immediate remedial action. It is, in the view of my delegation, essentially the duty of the Council to deal with such situations before they develop into full armed conflict. In the view of African States, the Council should impress upon the United Kingdom government the extreme undesirability of proceeding with the transfer of any armed forces to Southern Rhodesia until a government fully representative of the whole population, irrespective of race, creed or colour, has been established in accordance with resolution 1514 (XV). In particular, no major powers, which are generally recognised as the attributes of power and sovereignty, for example, the unrestricted right of taxation, should be transferred. In other words, there should be no taxation until there is representation. This aspect of the question should have potent meaning for the representative of the United States, whose forbears were the first to raise this cry – no taxation without representation.

Finally, let me make an appeal to the United Kingdom government. Do they not think that perhaps in the light of experience and in the light of what I have said here, their policy, the policy of attempting to hand over armed forces and a powerful army to the Southern Rhodesia government, has been mistaken? Forty years ago, the United Kingdom government proclaimed the Devonshire Declaration. They have never been able to implement it in regard to Southern Rhodesia. Ten years ago, against the advice of every African party and against the advice given by certain Commonwealth countries, they went ahead to set up the Federation. Today that Federation is in ruins. Might it not have been better if they had heeded African opinion then?

4

A NEW AFRICA

In March 1963, independence negotiations on the basis of the 1961 constitution were initiated by Winston Field, the Rhodesian prime minister. But as the discussions proceeded it soon became clear that there was fundamental disagreement between the British and Rhodesian governments. While the Rhodesian government maintained that it had 'general consent' for independence under the 1961 constitution, the British government insisted on satisfactory guarantees that:

   a. *there would be unimpeded progress to majority rule*
   b. *there would be no retrogressive amendments to the constitution to retard African advancement*
   c. *there would be immediate improvement in the political representation of Africans*
   d. *racial discrimination would end*
   e. *the basis of independence was acceptable to the people of Rhodesia as a whole*

The British government placed special emphasis on the fifth condition.

Unrest among Africans had been increasing ever since the break-up of the Federation at the end of 1963, and the arrest of African nationalist leaders. On January 1964, police opened fire on rioters in African townships near Salisbury, killing two and injuring many more. The shooting took place after a day of violence in which Africans set up road blocks. The police used tear gas and vomit gas to break up the crowds, and made many arrests. In March, among new measures brought in to deal with the growing number of demonstrations, whipping was introduced as punishment for throwing stones. There was already a maximum penalty of five years' imprisonment for offences of this kind. On 23 March 1964, prime minister Winston Field narrowly escaped death when a bomb exploded 100 yeards from him at a sports meeting in Bulawayo. The following month, on 13 April, Winston Field resigned, and was succeeded as prime minister by Ian Smith. As a correspondent of the Financial Times reported: 'The right wing has now taken over.'

At a press conference held on the day that he became prime minister, Ian Smith declared that the government of Rhodesia had no intention of weakening on the question of full independence. He said that the government would prefer a negotiated independence and would continue to strive for one: 'but we have made it quite clear that we can visualise circumstances which might drive us to do something else.'

The Reverend N. Sithole, president of ZANU, regarded the change of prime minister as a 'challenge to the African people'. He added: 'Now that the way is cleared for a unilateral declaration of independence', African people must gear themselves for an inevitable head-on collision.'

African unrest continued to grow, and on 17 April 1964 as tension rose, more than 28,000 police reservists were placed on eight hours' standby. In the Salisbury townships there were stonings, road blocks were set up, and police used tear gas to disperse demonstrators. In the centre of Salisbury, more than ninety women were arrested at a demonstration outside the British High Commission. This came the day after Ian Smith's blunt statement, at a press conference on 16 April, that he did not expect majority rule in Rhodesia in his lifetime. A month later, on 22 May, he went further and said: 'We will get our independence. . . . We must hold our ground and also try to regain some of the ground we were misled into giving away.'

This general pattern continued of growing determination among the African majority, and increasingly tough action on the part of the Smith government to suppress it; though it should be pointed out here that by no means all non-African Rhodesians opposed majority rule. On 28 May 1965, troops were called out to aid the police, and two large areas of Rhodesia, Nuanetsi and Lupane, were declared under a state of emergency. There were then about 1,000 Africans 'restricted' in Rhodesia.

The Rhodesian problem was the main topic of discussion at the Commonwealth Prime Minister's Conference held in London in July

1964. Before the conference opened, Nkrumah had private discussions with other African leaders and together they agreed a common line. In the official communique issued at the end of the conference on *15 July*, the prime ministers stated that:

a. they recognised the authority and responsibility of Britain for leading her remaining colonies to independence
b. the prime ministers would be unable to recognise any UDI
c. an independence conference should be convened which the leaders of all parties in Rhodesia should be free to attend. The object would be to seek agreement on the steps by which Rhodesia might proceed to independence within the Commonwealth at the earliest practicable time on the basis of majority rule

On his return to Accra, Nkrumah broadcast to the Ghanaian people: 'We managed to get the British government to agree to a conference of all political parties in Southern Rhodesia to work out a constitution based on majority rule. . . . Independent African states must continue to press the British government and the settler government of Southern Rhodesia if Africans are to succeed in liberating their brothers in Southern Rhodesia from minority oppression and rule.'

In September *1964*, Ian Smith and the British prime minister, Alex Douglas Home had discussions in London. Ian Smith pressed for independence on the basis of the existing constitution and franchise. The British prime minister restated the views expressed at the July conference of Commonwealth prime ministers and said that before granting independence, Britain must be satisfied that it was based on conditions acceptable to 'the people of the country as a whole'. Ian Smith accepted that there must be 'general consent' and said he was convinced that the majority of Rhodesians supported his request for independence on the basis of the existing constitution and franchise. He went on to say that he would consider how best to prove to the British that this was so.

There then arose the question of how to get an 'opinion' acceptable to the British government from Africans, the large majority of which did not qualify for a vote under the Rhodesian constitution. Furthermore, nothing had been agreed in the London talks between Home and Smith on the question of the release of imprisoned nationalists, and the removal of all restrictions to normal political activity.

Between 20 and 26 October *1964*, an indaba of 622 chiefs and headmen took place at Domboshawa, some twenty miles north of Salisbury. They were unanimous in their support of Ian Smith's call for independence under the existing constitution. But the British Labour government at once declared that it was unprepared to accept the decision of the chiefs as representing the wishes of the African population as a whole. Chiefs were appointed by the government, many of them having no hereditary claims. In some cases, chiefdoms had been reorganised for administrative convenience, and most chiefs could be expected to reflect the views of the government.

The British government's statement went on to explain the serious consequences of a UDI: 'A mere declaration of independence would have no constitutional effect. The only way Southern Rhodesia can become a sovereign independent state is by an Act of the British parliament. A declaration of independence will be an open act of defiance and rebellion and it would be treasonable to take steps to give effect to it.' The statement added that Rhodesians would cease to be British subjects, and 'the economic effects would be disastrous to the prosperity and prospects of the people of Rhodesia'.

On 5 November 1964, a referendum was held in Rhodesia. Voters were asked if they were 'in favour of Southern Rhodesia obtaining independence on the basis of the constitution of Southern Rhodesia 1961'. Some 58,176 voted 'Yes' and 6,101 voted 'No'. There were 944 spoilt papers. The overall percentage poll was 61·6 per cent and reflected the boycott of most of the African 'B' roll voters.

As might have been expected, the referendum failed to convince the British government or indeed world opinion, that it reflected the view of the mass of the people of Rhodesia. Accordingly, the British government proposed that an all-party parliamentary mission should visit Rhodesia to study the situation at first hand. In a statement on 21 January 1965, Ian Smith rejected the proposal, stating that the Rhodesian government was solely responsible for affairs within Rhodesia and could supply any information required by the British government. In February, however, Commonwealth Secretary, Arthur Bottomley, and Lord Chancellor, Lord Gardiner, arrived in Salisbury 'to get a cross-section of opinion within the country'. At an indaba held on 23 February, chiefs and headmen told Bottomley how they had been subjected to intimidation and violence. Bottomley sympathised and said that Britain would never recognise any unconstitutional action.

Bottomley then met ZAPU leader, Joshua Nkomo, who was living in the restriction camp at Gonakudzingwa. The latter rejected the 1961 constitution and demanded majority rule and the calling of a constitutional conference. During the following days, Bottomley and Gardiner proceeded to meet as many Rhodesians as possible from all walks of life to find out what they thought about Rhodesia's path to full independence. In a meeting with Dr M. I. Hirsch of the Reform Party, Bottomley said that the British government was not trying to bring about a one man one vote system as an immediate objective.

Commenting on the Bottomley–Gardiner mission, Ian Smith, in a radio interview on 4 March said that his government would not hesitate to declare UDI if it considered such a step necessary in the best interests of the country. Nkomo's comment on the mission was equally significant. He said that the British Labour government was apparently trying to buy time at the expense of the African nationalist movement in Rhodesia: 'The less Britain co-operates, the more hardened and resistant the Africans will become.' In Dar es Salaam, ZAPU representatives stated that Britain's acceptance of Smith's refusal of a constitutional conference was 'a signal to Africans to use means other than constitutional'.

In an effort to demonstrate support for his policies, Ian Smith called for a general election to be held on 7 May 1965. He wanted a two-thirds majority in parliament to strengthen his hand within Rhodesia's legislative machinery and in his negotiations with Britain. When nominations for the election closed on 14 April, 114 applications had been accepted, 78 for 'A' roll and 36 for 'B' roll seats.

The dialogue between the Smith government and the British government continued through the British High Commissioner in Rhodesia, J. B. Johnston. The Rhodesian elections had given the Rhodesian Front a clear victory. Out of a total of 68,384 votes cast, the Rhodesian Front gained 28,175 ('A' roll) and 206 ('B' roll); the Rhodesia Party 6,381 ('A' roll) and 505 ('B' roll); the Independents 964 ('A' roll) and 4 ('B' roll). There were 565 spoiled papers in the constituencies, and 3,622 in the electoral districts. Shortly afterwards, on 30 May, the Rhodesia Party announced a suspension of political activity since it was 'no longer possible to operate as a multi-racial party in parliament'. The ten African members of parliament formed themselves into the United People's Party (UPP), the official opposition.

On 25 June 1965, the Commonwealth Prime Ministers' Conference opened in London. On the initiative of Nkrumah, three African states, Kenya, Ghana and Sierra Leone called on the British government to set a specific date, and a time limit of three months for holding a constitutional conference. Dr Jawara, prime minister of Gambia, supported the move, but suggested a six month time limit. African leaders also demanded:

a. a declaration by the UK that its aim was to bring majority rule to Rhodesia
b. the release of all political prisoners in Rhodesia
c. the suspension of the 1961 constitution if they were not released
d. the formation of an interim government to repeal repressive laws and prepare for elections on the basis of one man one vote

Nkrumah emphasised that it was the purpose of the conference to end the racialist regime and not the prevention of UDI. He proposed that the conference should authorise the issue of a communique indicating the position from which they should all unanimously approach the Rhodesian question. In the final communique issued on 25 June 1965, the prime ministers welcomed the statement of the British government that the principle of one man one vote was regarded as the very basis of democracy and that this principle should apply to Rhodesia. The British government undertook to take full account in their discussions with the Smith government of all the views expressed at the conference, and to seek the calling of a constitutional conference as a natural step in Rhodesia's unimpeded progress to majority rule.

Ian Smith promptly announced that any attempt by the British government to convene a constitutional conference would be regarded as interference in the internal affairs of Rhodesia.

As on so many other vital occasions, Nkrumah was unable to get wholehearted support from other African states for a united, uncompromising stand on the Rhodesian issue. While in general supporting Nkrumah's demands, prime minister Milton Obote of Uganda was prepared to give Britain 'a reasonable time' in which to conclude negotiations with Salisbury. President Nyerere and the Tanzanian delegation were prepared to dissociate themselves from the part of the official communique concerning the time factor if the British government stated clearly that the object of the negotiations with the Smith government was to get independence on the basis of majority rule. On the other hand, President Kaunda of Zambia, called on the UK to impose a new democratic constitution on Rhodesia if necessary by force. Several African governments, including Ghana and Zambia offered facilities for Britain to use army bases in their countries for any use of force against the settler government. Ian Smith's reaction was to call the offer 'laughable'.

On 21 July 1965, the British minister of state for Commonwealth Relations, Cledwyn Hughes, arrived in Salisbury to pursue the dialogue with the Rhodesian government. He stayed a week, and before leaving Rhodesia said that 'some progress' had been made. The following month, on 6 August, Bottomley, on a visit to Ghana, assured Nkrumah that Britain would only grant independence to Rhodesia on the basis of majority rule. He said that Britain would not use force to impose a constitution on Rhodesia because it might lead to 'another Congolese situation', and would affect the economy of Zambia. Britain, he said, was working towards a development that could lead to majority rule in Rhodesia 'as speedily as possible'. If Rhodesia declared UDI, Britain would consider it illegal and impose economic sanctions. Some days later, in Nigeria, Bottomley blamed African nationalist leaders in Rhodesia for their failure to present a united front, and for refusing to contest elections.

On the first of September 1965, Ian Smith became more specific. He declared in parliament in Salisbury: 'We are going to have independence on the 1961 constitution. We believe this is imminent in the near future, and nothing will stop us.' On 29 September, two Rhodesian ministers, the minister for Internal Affairs and Public Service, and the minister of Finance arrived in London for talks. Ian Smith was not very optimistic about the success of their mission. He said he still hoped for a negotiated independence, but that if the talks failed the government would face up to the prospect of UDI. Accompanied by the minister of Justice and Order, Lardner-Burke, Ian Smith left Salisbury for London on 3 October for a final attempt to negotiate independence on the existing constitution.

In London, the prime ministers of Britain and Rhodesia proceeded with discussions on the 'five principles'. In expressing the views of the Rhodesian government, Ian Smith said that:

a. the 1961 constitution provided for increasing the African franchise. The question of guarantees against retrogression was essentially a matter of providing suitable mechanisms
b. the Rhodesian government proposed the addition of a senate to be composed of twelve chiefs elected by the Chief's Council. Members

of the senate would vote with the Assembly at third readings on any question affecting the revision of the entrenched clauses. This would replace the referendum procedure of the 1961 constitution

c. no increased representation of Africans in the Assembly was contemplated at present. But the Rhodesian government was prepared to consider extending the 'B' roll franchise to include all taxpayers

d. it was the wish of the Rhodesian government to see an end to racial discrimination

e. clear evidence had already been given of majority support in Rhodesia for independence on the basis of the 1961 constitution. This had been shown through consultation with tribal opinion and through the referendum

The Smith government proposals were unacceptable to the British government since they provided for no positive political and social advance for Africans. In particular, Harold Wilson rejected the idea that the chiefs represented the African majority in Rhodesia. In view of this 'no basis at present exists on which the British government would feel justified in granting independence to Rhodesia'.

On 14 October, Wilson proposed that a Commonwealth prime ministers' mission should visit Rhodesia. But Ian Smith rejected the idea, saying that the Rhodesian government could not commit itself to the decisions or recommendations of such a mission. Four days later, on 18 October, Wilson appealed to Ian Smith not to declare UDI 'for the sake of your country and for the sake of Africa'. In reply, Smith once again asked Britain to grant independence on the 1961 constitution, adding: 'This constitution covers your five principles if only you will admit it. . . . We have made our decision on what our next step should be. Its implementation and the consequences which flow from it now depend entirely on your response to this appeal which I now make to you at this eleventh hour.' Wilson replied on 21 October that there was never any understanding, implicit or explicit, that Rhodesia would be granted independence on the 1961 constitution without further change.

Meantime, the situation in Rhodesia and indeed the whole question of the liberation of southern Africa had become one of the major concerns of the Organisation of African Unity (OAU) formed in May 1963 largely as a result of Nkrumah's efforts. In the midnight speech made by Nkrumah at Ghana's independence on 6 March 1957, he had declared: 'The *independence of Ghana is meaningless unless it is linked up with the total liberation of the African continent.*' From then onwards, the Ghanaian government under his leadership, pursued an active Pan-African policy of support for liberation movements and for the unification of Africa. In May 1963, when the OAU was formed, it was Nkrumah's hope that with its embryo institutions and procedures for the total liberation and unification of Africa the stage was set for a great advance in the African Revolution. But the organisation did not develop in the way he hoped. He could not gain sufficient support among members for the setting up of an African High Command, so that right from the start the OAU lacked teeth. Nor could he get sufficient agreement on the question of forming an Executive Council, which he deemed the first step in the eventual formation of a Union Government of Africa. As he wrote of the OAU Charter in his last book* Revolutionary Path: *'It was a charter of intent rather than a charter of positive action. But this was inevitable in view of the widely differing policies of those who took part in the conference. All were agreed on the principles of African liberation and unification, and the need for close co-ordination and co-operation in economic, social and cultural spheres, but there were crucial differences of opinion when it came to questions of methods and procedures. . . . The OAU suffered from the start from inherent weaknesses. . . . As the years have passed, these fundamental differences of approach and emphasis, coupled with the stepping up of imperialist and neocolonialist pressures have led to compromise and delay in the OAU's handling of obstacles blocking the advance of the African Revolution. . . . In times of crisis it has failed to provide the dynamic leadership and decisive action expected of it. For example, the struggle in the Congo; the Nigerian civil war; UDI in Rhodesia; the question of South West Africa; the treatment of African political refugees; and problems arising from the rash of military coups which have taken place in recent years; all these, and other missed opportunities have shown the inherent weakness of an organisation which lacks cohesive political and military direction.'*

At the OAU Summit held in Addis Ababa in May 1964, a resolution was passed requesting Britain not to hand over sovereignty to the foreign minority in Rhodesia. The OAU, like the UN, held it to be the responsibility of Britain to see that independence for Rhodesia was only granted under conditions agreed by the Rhodesian people as a whole. But OAU resolutions proved as ineffective as those of the UN when it *came to exercising any meaningful effect on the slide to UDI in Rhodesia.*

When the OAU Summit Conference took place in Accra in October 1965, the subject of Rhodesia was once again high on the agenda. It was Nkrumah's hope that at last there would be agreement on the setting up of an Executive Council, for without effective political machinery the OAU could not hope to act effectively. In the words of Nkrumah: 'The OAU like the UN, was proving to be no better than the governments which controlled it, and the peoples whose interests it was formed to serve were in danger of being betrayed.' *But once again, after lengthy discussions, the OAU failed to set up either an Executive Council or an African High Command. Of the twenty-eight states which attended the conference, twenty-two voted for the proposal to form an Executive Council but a two-thirds vote, i.e. twenty-four of the total membership was needed, and it was therefore agreed that the proposal be referred back to the governments of the member states for further consideration and a report be submitted to the next session of the assembly. Nkrumah thereupon gave notice that he would place the setting up of an Executive Council as an amendment to the Charter of the OAU. There was agreement, however, on the question of Rhodesia. The resolution on Rhodesia, carried unanimously, is printed after the following full text of Nkrumah's speech at the opening session of the OAU Summit in Accra on 21 October 1965.*

Nkrumah's speech at the opening of the Summit Conference of the OAU in Accra, 21 October 1965

No honour is greater for me personally and for the government and people of Ghana than that we should have the privilege of extending to you, distinguished and eminent sons of Africa, our humble hospitality and sincere welcome.

I am particularly happy that I should have lived long enough to witness with you here the historic and momentous spectacle of this great assembly of the leaders and representatives of the independent states of Africa. We are glad to recall today memories of our struggles for independence; our prophetic imaginings of a new Africa emancipated from colonial chains, standing united and ready to play its historic role in world affairs. The dreams of generations are being steadily realised and fulfilled in many ways. Today, we raise our voices above the earth and to the world, not as the oppressed and down-trodden of mankind, but with the reborn dignity and strength of a people confident in themselves and certain of their future. It is in this spirit and with humility but with a sense of pride in our destiny that I stand before you to offer you, distinguished compatriots, a truly African welcome to Ghana.

Let me take this opportunity to welcome into our midst Brother Dawda Jawara, Prime Minister of the Gambia, who takes his seat among us for the first time. Gambia's accession to independence is of great significance to us because her independence closes the chapter of British and French colonialism in this part of our continent. Among us here also in the capacity of observers are the representatives of our courageous freedom fighters in the remaining territories of Africa still under the yoke of colonial rule.

On this historic occasion our minds must be filled with the suffering and heroism of our brothers in South Africa, Angola, Mozambique, Basutoland, Swaziland, Bechuanaland, South West Africa and the so-called Portuguese and Spanish possessions in Africa, whose mounting struggle for freedom and independence is also our struggle. Every minute, every moment, that passes sees the intensification of this struggle. Our freedom fighters refuse to bend their knees to colonial oppression. We salute them. Allow me to assure them in your name, that we stand by them; their struggle is our struggle, and we are determined that they shall soon come to share with us the benefits of freedom and independence, and the responsibilities of managing their own affairs in a united Africa.

The liberation of the whole of our continent, and the restoration of freedom and dignity to those of our brothers who are still under the colonial yoke remain our most important and immediate tasks, but we cannot forget that we are an integral part of humanity involved in all conflicts, perils, strivings and hopes of the human race all over the globe. We cannot ignore the fact that the same imperialist forces which exploit and subvert our independent states, and which exploit and oppress our peoples in the remaining colonial enclaves of Africa, are the very same forces which breed armed conflicts, civil strife and economic impoverishment on other continents.

It would be folly for us to dream of Africa as a peaceful and thriving continent in the midst of a world convulsed by armed conflicts, tormented by hunger and disease and continually menaced by imperialist intrigue and aggression. The armed conflict in Vietnam presents a grave peril to world peace. We must find a way to end that conflict permanently, if the world is to live in peace. In the same way, we must find the means to end the conflict over Kashmir permanently. We in Africa believe that the unhappy conflict between India and Pakistan can be of benefit to nobody except the imperialists, the colonialists and the neocolonialists. We must also find a way of putting an end to the current wave of aggression and armed conflicts which are today threatening the peace of the world and causing so much suffering.

We in Africa therefore demand the establishment of an atom free zone; we demand the ultimate destruction of nuclear stock-piles wherever they may be and the banning of their manufacture. On these and other issues we expect the world to respect our point of view, our stand, our heritage and our freedom and independence.

Brothers and colleagues, we are enjoined by the charter of the OAU to harness the material and human resources of our great and ancient continent for the well-being of all our people. From the experience of the last two years, are we sure that the charter as it stands at present contains adequate provisions to enable us to achieve this?

The people of Africa are waiting in anxious expectation for a concrete and constructive programme which will assist them to realise their hopes and aspirations. They know their suffering; they know how heavy is their burden and we who are here today must know too that if we fail them – woe betide us! It is true that all of us here are dedicated to the progress of Africa, and that we are determined to forge stronger bonds of unity in the interests of the welfare and happiness of the African people as a whole.

It is also true that a number of resolutions and declarations have been made and adopted, not only by our summit conference, but also by the Council of Ministers and by the various Commissions of the OAU. It is proper that we should have made and adopted these resolutions in the interests of African unity, but unless an effective political machinery is devised, to implement these resolutions, they remain no more than words on paper.

In spite of these resolutions and declarations, in spite of all good intentions, in spite of our plans, the naked fact, alas, is that Africa is still an impoverished continent, immobilised by the lack of political cohesion, harassed by imperialism and ransacked by neocolonialism. That is so because our unity is still incomplete and ineffective in the face of grave threats to our existence. What use is it to us then that our continent is so rich in material and human resources? Brothers and colleagues, the fault is in ourselves, not in our stars.

As I speak to you now the situation in Southern Rhodesia constitutes a grave threat to the peace of Africa. The racialist minority which has been allowed to assume power in this British colony now believes that its colonial constitution is not designed to enable it to introduce a complete version of apartheid in that colony. The racialist regime now threatens to take the law into its own hands and to make a unilateral declaration of independence. We recognise that Britain, as the metropolitan power bears the ultimate responsibility for the conduct of the colonial regime and for the maintenance of law and order in the colony. But we in Africa cannot remain indifferent to the fate of four million Africans in that territory, and cannot allow an extension of the vile, inhuman system of apartheid to other parts of Africa. We call on the British government to do its duty and to fulfil its obligations towards all the citizens in its colony of Southern Rhodesia. If armed force is required to bring the rebellious elements in the colony to order, we expect the United Kingdom government to use force to quell the rebellion. In the event of the United Kingdom government failing in its duty, I am sure that the member states of the OAU will take whatever steps are necessary in support of the four million Africans who form the majority in Southern Rhodesia.

Whatever the outcome of the present crisis, the struggle for the liberation of our brothers in Southern Rhodesia will not be abandoned by the Organisation of African Unity any more than it can be abandoned by the oppressed majority. We call on the British government to realise that the peace of Africa is immediately involved in the present crisis in Rhodesia and that the only safety and prosperity which the white settler minority can find is in a just and democratic constitution which allows the majority to rule for the benefit of all the people in the territory.

Another issue which requires our urgent attention at this conference is the problem of political refugees. Political refugees are a recent phenomenon in this continent, and they have arisen as an outcome of the struggle for independence. Indeed, so extensive is this question that there is perhaps not one independent African state today which has no political refugee problem. While in the fight against colonialism, we can expect a large measure of political cohesion and unity of purpose, what happens thereafter is a different matter. The responsibility for safeguarding political freedom, once it has been won, and the responsibility for fostering national development are not seen in the same light by those who only yesterday were colleagues and comrades-in-arms. Thus we find that Ivory Coast opposition elements come into hiding in Ghana; that Ghanaian dissidents go to live in Nigeria, Togo and the Ivory Coast. We find similar problems and difficulties virtually everywhere in Africa.

We are all aware of the international convention which recognises that any sovereign state can permit political refugees from another country to dwell in its territory. In a speech to the National Assembly on the Geneva Agreement which Ghana, and some other African states have ratified, I added an over-riding condition that they do not carry out on our soil political activities aimed against their own country. It would indeed be a sad reflection on our organisation, if even one African, whose well being and progress is the duty of everyone of us here, is permitted to wander around this continent, a reproach and a by-word among men, an outcast, deprived of food and shelter, a stateless individual, hounded from state to state, from country to country, without friends, and every man's hands against him.

As long as political boundaries persist in Africa, boundaries which we have inherited at independence and were drawn arbitrarily, with no heed to the ethnic, economic, and social realities of Africa, so long shall we be plagued by the political refugee problem. The political refugee problem is a social and political problem, and its only solution lies in an all-African Union Government within which our present boundaries will become links instead of barriers.

In the national constitution of Ghana, we have provision for the full or partial surrender of our sovereignty to an all-African Union. No member state should or can be expected to surrender its sovereignty for any lesser cause.

History is made only by bold ventures and not by retreating in the face of difficulties. Those who argue that the time is not ripe or that the difficulties are too great for the establishment of a continental Union Government are not recognising the imperative needs of the African continent or the overwhelming wishes and desires of the masses of the people of Africa.

We can delay no longer in taking the economic destiny of Africa into our own hands. Since the founding of the Organisation of African Unity at Addis Ababa, world trade has moved further and faster into the channels prepared by neocolonialism. The increased productivity of our wealthy continent has benefited not us, but the industrial nations. By depressing the prices of our raw materials and metals, they have stunted our economic progress. By raising the prices of their manufactured goods they have drained away any surpluses we might have acquired. The deliberate policy of neocolonialism emerges, not only to rob us of our wealth, but to prevent us from acquiring capital for our own development.

Those of us who are in the European Common Market and those of us outside it are equally rocked by economic storms and in danger of economic shipwreck. Everywhere in Africa, our economies are crumbling, our treasuries are getting empty, we are becoming client states, none of us can stand alone. We will remain in that condition until we take the economic and political destiny of Africa into our own hands. An African Common Market of three hundred million producers and consumers should have a productivity, a purchasing and bargaining power equal to any of those trading and currency blocs which now rule the commerce of the world.

Who is there to oppose or frustrate us, if we only have the courage to form an all-African Union Government? Can the industrialised nations do without our copper, our uranium, our iron ore, our bauxite, our coffee, cocoa, cotton, groundnuts, palm oil – or will they come running to us, as we have been running to them for trade on equitable terms? It is courage that we lack, not wealth.

It is true that we have made half-hearted attempts at economic co-operation, but without the drive and authority which can only come from political action. In this connection, let me quote the words of Brother Nyerere of Tanzania:

> 'For Africa, the lesson of our East African experience is that although economic co-operation can go a long way without political integration, there comes a point when movement must be either forward or backward – forward into, political decision or backward into reduced economic co-operation.'

The OAU must face such a choice now – we can either move forward to progress through an effective African Union or step backward into stagnation, instability and confusion – an easy prey for foreign intervention, interferences and subversion.

We have a market which can absorb the produce of modern giant enterprises. We have already through the efforts of the United Nations established an African Development Bank. There are recommendations adopted by the Addis Ababa summit conference as well as by the ECA concerning the establishment of a common monetary zone. What is left now is to create a Union Central Bank to back our individual currencies. The decision to create a Central Bank for Africa is a political one. Why is it that we are finding it difficult to take this decision in spite of so many resolutions, declarations and attempts? If Africa had one political front, a central machinery, such a decision would not be difficult to take and achieve.

Nothing that has happened since our Addis Ababa or Cairo meetings has caused me to alter my mind about the necessity of a Union Government for Africa. On the contrary, the growing perils in Africa and on the international scene, the growing strictures on world trade, the growing impoverishment of our primary producers, the persistent border disputes in Africa, the increasing instability caused by interference and subversive activities, the continued defiance and insolence of the racist minority regimes in South Africa and Southern Rhodesia – all these urge me to continue our pursuit for the political unification of Africa.

Our poverty, in the midst of our unbounded wealth; our weakness in spite of our unbounded might; the greatness of our need and the justice of our cause; the cry of our hungry and oppressed countrymen, as well as the courage and readiness to make further sacrifices by our liberation masses – all these urge me to restate my conviction that we must give political form or reality to our unity. I am more than ever convinced that Africa should unite into one state with a Union Government. This is the view which I stated at Addis Ababa in 1963 and in Cairo last year, and I still hold to this position.

It is clear from the shortcomings and difficulties experienced in the running of the OAU that it is necessary to strengthen the Charter of the OAU by providing an effective machinery which will enable us to work effectively and successfully for the realisation of our noble aims and objectives. Furthermore, the Heads of State and Government and the Council of Ministers cannot in practice meet as often as the imperative issues of a great continent demand.

I have never wavered in my conviction that the most effective form for the unity of Africa is a single African state, wielding its power through a Continental Union Government. In fact, everything that has happened since our first meeting in Addis Ababa has strengthened me in this conviction.

At the same time, in order to meet the views expressed by some of my brothers and colleagues, and to achieve as much unity as is possible now, I put forward the following proposals:

We should set up now a full-time body or Executive Council of the OAU to act as the Executive arm of the Assembly of the Heads of State and Government. The Assembly of Heads of

State and Government shall appoint from among themselves a chairman for the Executive Council which will be responsible for implementing the decisions of the Assembly of Heads of State and Government.

I also propose that this body shall be responsible for initiating policies and making recommendations to the Assembly of Heads of State and Government on matters pertaining to the aims and objectives of the OAU as set out in Article Two of the Charter.

Under my proposals, the Assembly of Heads of State and Government shall continue to be the supreme governing body of the OAU as in article eight of our charter. I further propose that the Assembly shall elect a Union president and a number of Union vice-presidents to meet periodically during the ensuing year in order to review the work of the Executive Council when the Assembly is not in session.

The General Secretariat of the OAU shall be the Secretariat of the Executive Council.

I am confident, brothers and colleagues, that from our deliberations we shall leave yet another significant mark on the history of our times. A united Africa is destined to be a great force in world affairs. So the battle is joined, and we cannot disengage, until the wishes and aspirations of our people have been met. Just as in the 1950's we stood abreast and solid in the vanguard of Africa's liberation movement, so in the 1960's we shall see an even greater struggle for the fruits of the African revolution – a new and unified society without which the peoples of Africa cannot independently survive or prosper: Africa shall be a bright star among the constellation of nations.

Resolution carried unanimously at the OAU Summit in Accra, October 1965

The Assembly of Heads of State and Government meeting in Accra, Ghana, from October 21 to 25, 1965;

Deeply concerned by the gravity of the situation in Southern Rhodesia;

Considering that the situation constitutes a serious threat to world peace;

Noting:

a. the statement of the United Kingdom Government that it will regard any Unilateral Declaration of Independence made by the European minority in Southern Rhodesia as illegal and amounting to an act of rebellion and treason punishable by the mere imposition of economic sanctions and non-recognition

b. the recent United Nations resolution passed with an overwhelming majority calling on the United Kingdom Government to take all possible steps to prevent Unilateral Declaration of Independence and pledging support for any future measures that the United Nations might decide upon in this matter

The Heads of State and Government of the OAU

Deplore the refusal of the United Kingdom to meet with firmness and resoluteness the threat of Unilateral Declaration of Independence by a European minority Government. Deplore moreover the refusal of the United Kingdom Government to state categorically that it will not grant independence to Rhodesia except on the basis of a majority government;

Call upon:

1. The United Nations to regard any such declaration of unilateral independence as constituting a threat to international peace, and to take any steps that such a situation requires in accordance with the Charter and to help to establish a majority government in Southern Rhodesia;

2. The United Kindom Government, the administering power having the responsibility of administration and having the sole responsibility for the present situation:

a. to suspend the 1961 Constitution of Southern Rhodesia forthwith and to take all measures necessary including the use of armed forces to take over the administration of the territory

b. to release the leaders of the nationalist movements, Joshua Nkomo, Sithole, and other political prisoners *c.* to hold a constitutional conference with the participation of the representatives of the entire population of Southern Rhodesia with a view to adopting a new Constitution guaranteeing universal adult suffrage (one man, one vote), free elections and independence

3. *Calls upon* all governments and international bodies in the event of a unilateral declaration of independence to withhold recognition of a European minority government, and to apply sanctions;

4. *Declare* all OAU member States, in the event of failure on the part of the United Kingdom, to take in time the measures set forth in operative paragraph 2a:

   a. to reconsider all political, economic, diplomatic and financial relations with the Government of the United Kingdom of Great Britain and Northern Ireland in the event of this Government granting and tolerating the independence of Rhodesia under a minority Government
   b. to use all possible means, including the use of force, with the view to opposing a unilateral declaration of independence
   c. to give immediate and every necessary assistance to the people of Zimbabwe with the view to establishing a majority government in the country

5. *Empowers* the African Group at the United Nations to ensure that the request sent to the United Nations and the Security Council receives due consideration.

5

ONE MAN ONE VOTE

In an attempt to break the deadlock, British prime minister, Harold Wilson flew to Salisbury on 25 October 1965. On his arrival in Rhodesia he said that he and Ian Smith would discuss the 'fifth principle', that a solution must be acceptable to the people of Rhodesia as a whole. Right from the start of the discussions, Wilson made it clear that the British government:

a. *would not use 'military power' to achieve a solution to Rhodesia's constitutional problems*
b. *did not believe that majority rule could be achieved 'today or tomorrow'*
c. *considered that Rhodesian Africans should unite to work out a constitutional settlement; and that they should register and vote in elections*

At first it seemed that no agreement would be reached. But just before he left Salisbury on 29 October, the two prime ministers agreed on a procedure by which African opinion could be consulted. A Royal Commission was to be established under the chairmanship of Sir Hugh Beadle, the Chief Justice of Rhodesia, to look into the question of independence. The Commission's terms of reference, however, had still to be agreed. The British government wanted the Commission to recommend amendments to the 1961 constitution which would provide a basis for independence acceptable to the people of Rhodesia as a whole. But the Smith government thought that the Commission should receive from the two governments an agreed draft independence arrangement based on the 1961 constitution with such amendments as might be considered necessary; and that the Commission should then proceed to find out whether such a document was acceptable to the Rhodesian people as a whole. Two of the main points at issue between the two governments were the doctrine of the so-called blocking third, or blocking quarter, for amendments to the constitution of clauses which were not entrenched; and the provision of effective safeguards for the specially entrenched clauses.

When news of the proposed Royal Commission reached Ghana, Nkrumah made it clear that his government strongly objected to the suggestion. He described it as a 'betrayal of the four million unrepresented African inhabitants of the colony'. The stand of the Ghana government was supported by a Kenya government statement declaring that there could be no permanent solution in Rhodesia which was not based on majority rule. In Rhodesia, Joshua Nkomo and the Reverend Sithole both condemned the proposed Royal Commission, referring to it as 'a time wasting device'.

On leaving Salisbury, Harold Wilson flew back to the UK via Ghana where he had an important discussion with President Nkrumah at Accra airport. The meeting took place on 31 October, just six days after the ending of the Accra OAU Summit, and the passing of the strongly worded resolution on Rhodesia.* In choosing to visit Accra rather than any other African capital, Wilson acknowledged Nkrumah's leadership, and his dominant role in the stand taken by the African independent states in support of the African majority in Rhodesia.

In a prepared statement, Nkrumah left Wilson in no doubt about his government's stand on the Rhodesia issue, and particularly on the question of the Royal Commission. Nkrumah's prepared statement of 31 October 1965; a statement summarising the position of the Ghana government on the Rhodesian issue; and a personal message from Nkrumah to Wilson dated 2 November 1965, were subsequently printed in Ghana and published as a government pamphlet under the title One man one vote.

It was always the policy of Nkrumah to have the texts of all important policy statements published and distributed by the government printer, not only to keep the people fully informed, but for record purposes. In the case of One man one vote there was an additional reason. On reaching London airport, Wilson told the press that Nkrumah had expressed his

* See pp. 73–75.

views on the Rhodesian question from prepared notes, thereby implying that Nkrumah might have spoken differently if he had first heard what Wilson had to say. Nkrumah in his message to Wilson of 2 November quickly disabused him of this idea: 'Nothing which you told me changed in any way my views on the situation in Southern Rhodesia on your proposals for the setting up of a Royal Commission.' After restating his stand, Nkrumah ended: 'In view of the misunderstanding of my position, which may have arisen out of your comments to the press on what I said in Accra, I am publishing this message so that my stand may be made perfectly clear.'

Views expressed by Nkrumah in discussions with the British prime minister, Harold Wilson, in Accra on 31 October 1965

As unfortunately the time at our disposal is limited, I thought it might be best if I began by speaking frankly about the Southern Rhodesian situation as I see it. I have made a note of the essence of what I am going to say and it may be convenient if I let you have a copy of this. I intend subsequently to make public the views I have expressed.

There is no need for me to describe in detail the shortcomings of the 1961 Rhodesian constitution. I agree with all the criticisms which the British Labour Party then made. The official spokesman of the British Labour Party asked the British parliament to condemn it on the ground that it was a bad constitution, and I need not go into details of debates at which both you, Mr Prime Minister, and you, Sir Elwyn, were present. I would like, however, to remind you of what was said by Mr Dugdale who had been the Minister of State for Colonial Affairs in Lord Attlee's administration. He quoted the verdict of the Roman Catholic Archbishop and Bishops of Southern Rhodesia. You will remember he gave details of the account which they gave in a pastoral letter as to the appalling conditions of the African people of the colony and he quoted their conclusion in which they said: 'Such a state of affairs cries to heaven for vengeance and even in the natural order can only breed crime and chaos.'

Quite frankly after the wholesale condemnation of this constitution, I am unable to understand why apparently the

British government are now trying to persuade the African people of the colony to work this constitution. The British Labour Party quite rightly, in my view, denounced it in 1961 root and branch. You will remember that the safeguards against discrimination which it provides were described by the present British Home Secretary as 'very nearly illusory'. You will remember he concluded by saying: 'I hope I do not exaggerate my language. I have considered it carefully.'

I must say that in my view the racial discrimination in Southern Rhodesia is, as the British Chancellor of the Exchequer said when condemning in the British parliament the 1961 constitution, on a par with that of South Africa. You will remember that he said: 'To go to Bulawayo or to Fort Victoria is to feel oneself in South Africa.' I myself consider that what he said is only the bare truth. The discrimination against the African population of the colony is among the most barbarous, shameful and disgusting in the world. It has been described by speaker after speaker in the British House of Commons and I am sure that therefore there is no need to labour further the point.

I would like, however, to say something about how present negotiations in Southern Rhodesia appear to me to match up with the decisions which we all came to at the last Commonwealth Prime Ministers' Conference. If I may begin by quoting one of the first paragraphs in our final communique to which we all agreed unanimously. Let me read it:

'The Prime Ministers recognised that the Commonwealth, as a multi-racial association, is opposed to discrimination on grounds of race or colour; and they took the opportunity of their meeting to reaffirm the declaration in their communique of 1964 that, 'for all Commonwealth governments, it should be an objective of policy to build in each country a structure of society which offers equal opportunity and non-discrimination for all its peoples, irrespective of race, colour or creed. The Commonwealth should be able to exercise constructive leadership in the application of democratic principles in a manner which will enable the people of each country of different racial and cultural groups to exist and develop as free and equal citizens".'

Quite frankly, I cannot see how the present negotiations in

Southern Rhodesia fit in with this statement of principle. I am compelled to say that it seems to me that they are aimed primarily at finding a formula under which the existing constitution can be allowed to continue in being. As I see it the issue of a unilateral declaration of independence is only one aspect of the matter. The settler regime only wishes for independence so that they can be assured that they can continue unimpeded their present policy of suppression and exploitation of the African population. If the British government is prepared to abandon the principle set out in our communique then, of course, the settlers would agree. It seems to me that the compromise which is at present being suggested is that there should be agreement on a constitution which would be merely a modified form of the 1961 constitution.

It is my duty to issue a serious warning as to the grave consequences which would flow from any attempt by the British government to set up a racialist state in the heart of Africa. The test that we should apply is whether or not the state is based on racial principles. If it is based on racial principles then our attitude to it would be the same whether it was declared unilaterally or whether it was set up by an Act of the British parliament. I am certain that it is the view of all African states that under no circumstances could they permit a second South Africa to be established in the African continent. Therefore, irrespective of whether such a state was established by unilateral action or by the Act of British parliament, African states would be forced to oppose it in one form or the other, if necessary. In view of the trend of negotiations in Southern Rhodesia, I consider that it is necessary for the African states now to start making practical plans as to how they can deal militarily, if necessary, with the situation. I hope that you will appreciate that I speak with a full sense of responsibility and realising the grave issues involved.

In any event, I would like to make it absolutely clear that Ghana would not recognise any independent state set up in Southern Rhodesia unless that state was based on the principle of majority rule. Irrespective of whether it was created by an Act of the British parliament or unilaterally by the settlers, Ghana would oppose its entry into the Commonwealth, the

United Nations and all other international bodies. If the British parliament were to provide that the British crown should be the titular sovereign of a racial independent Southern Rhodesia then Ghana would no longer be able to recognise the British crown as head of the Commonwealth.

My Government stands firmly by the resolution on Southern Rhodesia unanimously adopted by the Assembly of African Heads of State and Government which met last week in Accra. Among other things this resolution declared that the United Kingdom government as the administering power having the sole responsibility for the present situation in Southern Rhodesia, should do the following three things. First, the British government should suspend the 1961 constitution which has, of course, been condemned not only by the British Labour Party but also by the United Nations. The British government should also take all measures necessary, including the use of armed force, if required, so as to take over the administration of the colony. Secondly, the resolution asks that the British government should secure the release of the nationalist leaders, Mr Joshua Nkomo and the Rev. Sithole, and the many others who are imprisoned or restricted because of their advocacy of justice for the African inhabitants of the colony. In regard to this part of the resolution, I should mention that at our Commonwealth Prime Ministers' meeting an appeal was also made and recorded in our communique 'for the immediate release of all detained or restricted African leaders as a first step to diminishing tension and preparing the way for a Constitutional Conference'. I much regret that not only has this appeal gone unheeded but that the British prime minister does not appear even to have brought it to the notice of the Southern Rhodesian authorities during his recent visit. To my mind, it is quite illogical to appeal on the one hand to the African leaders to adopt constitutional methods and not to appeal on the other hand to the settler regime to release them from restriction.

The third point of the resolution of the Organisation of African Unity was that the British government should hold a constitutional conference with a view to the participation of the representatives of the entire population of Southern Rhodesia with a view to adopting a new constitution guaranteeing universal adult suffrage on the basis of one man one vote, free elections and national independence.

In connection with this point of the resolution, I must refer again to another undertaking which the British government gave to us at the prime ministers' meeting. Our final communique recorded that in the process 'of seeking to reach agreement on Rhodesia's advance to independence a constitutional conference would, at the appropriate time be a natural step'. The communique went on to record the promise of the British government that if discussions did not develop satisfactorily in this direction in a reasonably speedy time the British government would be ready to consider promoting a constitutional conference in order to ensure Rhodesia's progress to independence on a basis acceptable to the people of Rhodesia as a whole. I cannot consider that the proposed Royal Commission which is to be composed of three individuals, two of whom come from the settler regime and one of whom is nominated by the British government, is in anyway an adequate substitute for the constitutional conference.

To my mind one of the most serious aspects of the present Southern Rhodesian situation is that the British government appear to me to have gone back on the solemn undertakings which they gave to the Heads of Government of the Commonwealth. I remember very well that at the Prime Ministers' Conference, we were assured that the British government would, whatever happened, stick to the principle of one man one vote in regard to Southern Rhodesia. In case it is suggested my recollection is at fault, let me quote from our final communique. The passage concerned reads as follows: 'In this connection they' – that is to say the other Heads of Government of the Commonwealth – 'welcome the statement of the British government that the principle of "one man one vote" was regarded as the very basis of democracy and this should be applied to Rhodesia.'

I am bound to say that from everything which has been published about the present negotiations it appears that the British government has abandoned this vital principle and is prepared to go back on its solemn undertaking to the Commonwealth

Heads of Government. I hope I am wrong about this and that the British government will make it clear that they stand by the undertaking which they gave to the Commonwealth. Before concluding these remarks, there is one other matter to which I must refer, and that is the announced refusal of the British government under any circumstances to use armed force in Southern Rhodesia. I am astounded that the British government should have said that they would not give armed protection in the event of a unilateral declaration of independence to those in Rhodesia who resisted an illegal seizure of power. So far as I know this is the first time in history that any country, great or small, has declared in advance that those who are prepared to risk their lives in defending the legal government will receive no support from the forces of law and order of the country against whom the revolt is directed.

Ghana government statement issued on 31 October, 1965

Osagyefo the President received the British Prime Minister, Mr Harold Wilson, at Accra airport this morning. During this meeting the Southern Rhodesian issue was discussed. Osagyefo the President made clear to the British Prime Minister the position of the Government of Ghana on this issue which may be summarised as follows:

1. The government of Ghana stands firmly by the resolution on Southern Rhodesia passed recently by the Assembly of African Heads of State and Government, in which the United Kingdom government, the administering power having the sole responsibility for the present situation in Southern Rhodesia, is called upon:
   - *a.* to suspend the 1961 constitution of Southern Rhodesia forthwith and to take all measures necessary including the use of armed force to take over the administration of the territory
   - *b.* to release the leaders of the nationalist movements, Joshua Nkomo, Sithole and other political prisoners
   - *c.* to hold a constitutional conference with the participation

of the representatives of the entire population of Southern Rhodesia with a view to adopting a new constitution guaranteeing universal adult suffrage (one man, one vote), free elections and independence.

2. Accordingly, the government of Ghana considers that the proposed appointment of a Royal Commission composed of two settler nominees and one nominee of the British government to inquire into the best means of consulting the Rhodesian people on the proposed constitution, is a betrayal of the four million unrepresented African inhabitants of the colony, and is merely a device to sidetrack an issue which cannot be left unsolved any longer without it becoming a danger to world peace.

3. The attention of the British Prime Minister was drawn to the British statement to the recent Commonwealth Conference that they accepted the principle of one man one vote as the very basis of democracy and undertook to apply this principle in Southern Rhodesia. Osagyefo emphasized that this principle must be applied in Southern Rhodesia.

4. In the event of the British government refusing to act in accordance with this principle, the African states would have no alternative but to take whatever steps would be necessary in support of the four million Africans who form the majority in Southern Rhodesia.

Message from Nkrumah to Wilson of 2 November, 1965

You said to the press at London airport that my views on the proposed Southern Rhodesian Royal Commission were contained in notes prepared before your arrival. From this you implied that I would not have made such criticisms if I had heard your arguments. Naturally, as the time at our disposal was so short, I had prepared for you notes of my views on the Southern Rhodesian question. I only gave these notes to you after I heard and considered what you had to say. Nothing which you told me changed in any way my views on the situation in Southern Rhodesia and on your proposals for the setting up of a Royal Commission.

ONE MAN ONE VOTE

What you are suggesting is that there shall be a Royal Commission of three Europeans with a built-in settler majority to determine under what constitution the four million Africans of Southern Rhodesia shall be governed. The British government has a duty to protect the African inhabitants of Southern Rhodesia. The United Kingdom has, nevertheless, agreed to a proposal that most important questions of principle shall be decided by a body on which Britain has not even a majority and from which all Africans are excluded. It was for this reason that my government described this scheme as a betrayal of the four million Africans of the colony.

I am not even sure that your views of the impartiality of the chairman, whom Ian Smith has nominated, are borne out by the facts. Sir Hugh Beadle's long record as a settler representative in the colony's Legislative Assembly and his many anti-African statements and acts are known. As successively Minister of Justice, of Internal Affairs, of Health and of Education, he enforced hostile anti-African legislation. In 1949 he was appointed by the settlers of the area which afterwards comprised the Rhodesian Federation to represent to the then British government that not only the Africans of Southern Rhodesia but also those of Zambia and Malawi wished to be ruled by an all-white parliament when the Federation was established. Under these circumstances, it is very difficult to have any confidence in Sir Hugh Beadle's impartiality.

At the Prime Ministers' Conference, it was recorded in our communique that the Heads of Government of the other Commonwealth countries 'welcomed the statement of the British government that the principle of "one man one vote" was regarded as the very basis of democracy and this should be applied to Rhodesia'. The discussions at the Commonwealth Conference on Southern Rhodesia accepted this fundamental principle as a basis for action by the British government. I cannot reconcile this declaration with your more recent statement that the African population of Southern Rhodesia cannot hope for majority rule today or tomorrow. Apparently your government now takes the view that African capacity to rule stops short at the Zambesi and that while those north of the river are perfectly capable of running their own state, those immediately south of it lack the ability to do so. I fear that to come to such a conclusion is merely to accept the racialist theories of the present settler regime.

The proposals now being made in regard to Southern Rhodesia, as I understand them, appear to me to be a breach of the various undertakings which the British government gave the Commonwealth Heads of Government at that meeting. Not only did the British government say that there must be progressive elimination of racial discrimination and unimpeded progress to majority rule but they emphasised that these must be guaranteed. What is now apparently being suggested is that these principles can be secured by including them in some constitution under which the colony will be given independence. This is no better than what the British parliament did in the case of South Africa.

How can it be supposed for one moment that the present settler regime, which is threatening to overturn by force the existing constitution, even before the country is independent, would after independence respect any guarantees in the constitution. The only reason why the settlers are seeking independence is that they wish by this means to establish a racialist state and to do away with all African progress towards majority rule. It is obvious that the only way in which the principles laid down at the Commonwealth Conference can be achieved is by the establishment of a government based upon "one man one vote".

You also said to the British press that I believed that the only solution to the Southern Rhodesian problem was the use of force by Britain. Successive British governments have, time and time again, insisted that the authority and responsibility for Southern Rhodesia rests exclusively with the United Kingdom government. If, therefore, force has to be used it is Britain's responsibility to use it. Two years ago at the Security Council the United Kingdom government vetoed a resolution which would have prevented the arming of the settlers. In consequence, Southern Rhodesia has now been equipped with the most modern weapons, including a powerful air force.

ONE MAN ONE VOTE

I agree, however, with President Kaunda that the settlers would not use these forces against British troops. In my view it is only necessary for the British government to show that it is prepared, if necessary, to use force in order to secure a peaceful solution. In any event, if the British government rules out the use of force, it should be made quite clear to the settlers that they too will receive no assistance from Britain in the event of a revolt by the African population.

At the last Commonwealth Conference we all agreed that in the process of seeking to reach agreement on Rhodesia's advance to independence a constitutional conference would, at the appropriate time, be a natural step. Your government said that if discussions with the settlers did not develop satisfactorily in a reasonably speedy time then the United Kindom government 'would be ready to consider promoting such a conference in order to ensure Rhodesia's progress to independence on a basis acceptable to the people of Rhodesia as a whole'. It seems to me that the time has clearly come when such a conference should be called.

Finally, I must beg you to think again. It would indeed be a tragedy if the Commonwealth were to be destroyed on the issue of placating some 217,000 white settlers, the majority of whom have only established themselves in Rhodesia since the last world war.

In view of the misunderstanding of my position, which may have arisen out of your comments to the press on what I said in Accra, I am publishing this message so that my stand may be made perfectly clear.

6

MOCKERY OF DEMOCRACY

In a broadcast to the Rhodesian people on 2 November 1965, Ian Smith declared that the proposal for a Royal Commission provided the 'one possible chance' of a negotiated settlement. But he went on to remark that the differences between the two governments were as 'irreconcilable as ever'.

On 5 November 1965, a state of emergency was declared in Rhodesia. Two days later, in a last attempt to reach a settlement, Wilson proposed that he and Ian Smith should meet in Malta for further talks. He suggested that the Chief Justice of Rhodesia, Sir Hugh Beadle, should fly to London immediately to discuss how the Royal Commission would operate in view of the state of emergency in Rhodesia.

Speaking in Salisbury on 8 November, Ian Smith rejected the proposal for a meeting with Wilson in Malta, repeating that the views of the two governments were 'irreconcilable'. But on the morning of 11 November, Wilson telephoned Smith in an effort to resolve the disagreement over the proposed Royal Commission, and during the course of their discussions he offered to send a senior minister to Rhodesia immediately.

It was later on the same day, 11 November 1965, that Ian Smith broadcast to the nation the Rhodesian government's proclamation of independence (UDI). Immediately following the declaration of independence, the Governor of Rhodesia, Sir Humphrey Gibbs, announced that he had been instructed by the Queen to suspend Ian Smith and his government. But the announcement was not published in Rhodesia due to the imposition of censorship. Meantime, a new constitution described as 'interim' was introduced. In essence the 1965 constitution asserted

Rhodesian independence and repudiated British authority, though in some ways it was similar to the 1961 constitution. The proportion and number of constituencies and electoral districts ('A' and 'B' roll seats) and delimitation provisions were retained. Electoral laws, franchise qualifications and provisions for the Constitutional Council and for safeguards concerning land legislation were practically the same. But the new constitution contained provisions validating UDI and removing limitations on Rhodesia's sovereignty. There was no longer provision for appeal to the Privy Council, and the Governor was replaced by a Head of State designated Officer administering the government. On 17 November 1965, C. W. Dupont was sworn in as the first acting officer administering the government.

Interrupting its general debate, the plenary session of the UN General Assembly condemned UDI and called on Britain to take the necessary steps to end the rebellion. The resolution was approved by 107 votes in favour to 2 against (Portugal and South Africa). France abstained, and Britain did not participate in the voting stating that the British Foreign Secretary was en route to New York and would report direct to the Security Council on the following day.

Harold Wilson in a statement in parliament on 12 November, condemned UDI as illegal and an act of rebellion. He called upon Rhodesians to remain loyal to the Queen and the law of the land, adding: 'We shall have no dealings with the rebel regime.'

Reaction to UDI among the independent states of Africa was immediately and strongly expressed. Prime minister Milton Obote of Uganda proposed an urgent meeting of leaders of East Africa and Zambia to discuss the situation. On 15 November, a meeting attended by President Kenyatta of Kenya, President Nyerere of Tanzania, prime minister Milton Obote of Uganda, and the vice-president of Zambia, Mr Kamanga was held in Nairobi. The leaders agreed on a line of action to help Africans in Rhodesia and the people of Zambia, the country most likely to suffer from the effects of UDI. The object was not to help Britain to re-establish her authority in Rhodesia, but to assist Africans to achieve their independence, and to help Zambia overcome severe economic pressures resulting from UDI.

In Accra, President Nkrumah issued a government statement on 11 November as soon as UDI had been declared by the Smith government. He called upon Britain to suppress the rebellion, and for members of the OAU *to implement effectively the resolution on Rhodesia passed at the October 1965 OAU Summit meeting in Accra. The full text follows of the Ghana government's call for 'positive action' to end the rebellion by the settler government in Rhodesia.*

Ghana government statement on UDI, 11 November 1965

The government of Ghana welcomes the decision of the British government to refer the Rhodesian issue to the Security Council of the United Nations. It regrets however that the British government proposes that the Council should limit the exercise of its authority to economic sanctions. In the view of the government of Ghana, the first Act of the Council should be to rectify the situation created by Britain when, two years ago, the United Kingdom government vetoed a resolution of the Council, proposed on the initiative of Ghana and supported by all African states, and which would have effectively prevented the arming of the white minority in Southern Rhodesia. The permanent members of the Security Council have quite sufficient forces at their disposal to destroy the Rhodesian air force and army in a matter of minutes. They have a moral obligation to use their forces in order to redress the wrong, which United Kingdom government did when she vetoed the resolution of the Council which would otherwise have deprived the settlers of the armed forces on which they now rely. In the view of the government of Ghana, the present illegal and treasonable declaration of independence, flows directly from the United Kingdom government's veto of the Security Council's resolution in September, 1963. It was by this veto that Britain provided the settlers with the armed forces which they now use to defy British authority and to threaten the African continent with a racial war. The United Kingdom has therefore a particular duty to do everything possible to redress the wrong which she did on this occasion. At the very least, Britain should recall immediately all United Kingdom subjects serving in the Rhodesian army, air force and police; and the Security Council should order South Africa to do the same in regard to their own citizens. It is

MOCKERY OF DEMOCRACY

a myth to say that such a thing as a Southern Rhodesia air force, army or police force exists. Except where African personnel is employed in a menial capacity these forces are composed almost exclusively of British and South African citizens and their recall would leave the Southern Rhodesian rebels powerless.

It seems to the government of Ghana that two hundred thousand settlers living amidst a population of four million Africans would never have declared unilateral independence unless they had received in advance powerful secret backing from certain quarters. It must be obvious that Smith would not have acted as he did unless he had received secret assurances from South Africa and from Portugal. In the view of the government of Ghana, the United Kingdom government and the Security Council can only end this rebellion in Southern Rhodesia if they take appropriate and speedy action against all involved. To the government of Ghana it seems clear that an international complex of financial interests which derive their profits from the exploitation of the African people are actively engaged in supporting the treasonable and treacherous Smith regime and that unless the Commonwealth, the Security Council and the Organisation of African Unity act quickly to deal boldly with the Southern Rhodesian rebellion, no other solution would be effective and the southern part of Africa would pass into the hands of the most vicious racialists which have yet been seen.

The government of Ghana regrets that the British government has merely contented itself with dismissing Ian Smith and his regime and invoking economic sanctions. In the view of the government of Ghana it was the duty of the British government to have taken this step before Smith completed his act of rebellion and in its view the rebellion might have been prevented had the British government been prepared to act with courage and determination at an earlier stage. However this may be, in the government of Ghana's opinion, the important thing to do is not to make a mere gesture by dismissing Smith at this stage but instead to revoke forthwith the 1961 constitution which has already been condemned by the United Nations, the Organisation of African Unity and by a large majority of the Commonwealth. Ghana considers that, immediately this constitution is revoked, the British government should call a constitutional conference which in any event it promised to do if negotiation with the settler regime proved unsatisfactory. At this constitutional conference all political parties, except those in active rebellion against the British government should be represented. A new constitution should be established providing for majority rule. The British government should give legislative effect to the new Rhodesian constitution and support to the Zimbabwe government thereafter set up. In accordance with the OAU resolution, the government of Ghana would give every support to such a government and hopes that powers outside the African continent would do likewise.

The government of Ghana is much concerned over the fate of those in the colony of Southern Rhodesia who have refused to join in the revolt of the settler regime. It notes with dismay that in the statement made by the British prime minister in the House of Commons no provision is apparently made for lending protection to the Governor or to those members of judiciary, armed forces or to the police who refuse to accept Smith's treasonable seizure of power.

The government of Ghana has taken note of the fact that the United Kingdom government still maintains that Southern Rhodesia is a British colony and that it is the exclusive responsibility of the United Kingdom government. This involves Britain taking positive action right now to deal with this rebellion.

The Organisation of African Unity has charted the course during its last Summit Meeting in Accra, in the event of the illegal seizure of power by the Smith regime. It is therefore the clear duty of all progressive and peace-loving states in the world, and particularly the non-aligned countries, to aid the OAU in ensuring the effective implementation of its resolution on Southern Rhodesia.

7

THREAT TO AFRICA

On the day that UDI was declared, the British government imposed economic sanctions. Rhodesia was expelled from the sterling area and Commonwealth preference on purchases of Rhodesian goods was ended. In addition, a complete ban was placed on purchases by Britons of Rhodesian tobacco or sugar. All trade with Rhodesia was made subject to exchange control; and exports to Rhodesia could no longer be financed through the Export Credits Guarantee Department.

Further sanctions were imposed by the British government on 1 December 1965. Transfers from British firms to Rhodesian subsidiaries (including banks) was forbidden. The payment of dividends and interest, and of pensions to Rhodesian residents was to be into blocked accounts in London. The Board of the Reserve Bank of Rhodesia was dismissed and replaced by a British Board. British banks were forbidden to finance trade between Rhodesia and third countries. Finally, on 17 December, Britain imposed a complete ban on the sale of oil by British firms to Rhodesia.

Meantime, other governments had also been imposing trade sanctions in compliance with a UN Security Council resolution of 19 November calling for a complete economic embargo of Rhodesia. The resolution condemned 'the usurpation of power by a racist settler minority', and called on Britain to end the rebellion. It also called on all states not to recognise the illegal government of Rhodesia and 'to do their utmost' in order to break all economic relations with Rhodesia including an embargo on oil and petroleum products. The vote was ten in favour of the resolution and none against, with France abstaining.

As Harold Wilson had openly stated before UDI, the British government had no intention of using force to bring down the Smith government. But this did not rule out the possibility of sending help to Zambia. On 12 November 1965, the day after UDI, Zambian and Rhodesian troops moved up to their common frontier, and President Kaunda asked Britain to send troops to protect the power supply at Kariba if the Smith government threatened to cut off electricity to the Zambian copperbelt. The British special envoy on east and central Africa, Malcolm Macdonald, flew to Lusaka to discuss the question. He was followed on 2 December by Arthur Bottomley who informed Kaunda that Britain would send Royal Air Force planes and personnel for the air defence of Zambia; but that there would have to be further discussion on the question of land forces.

No one could be in doubt any longer of the fact that Britain would not use force in Rhodesia. The rebel government was well armed, due to the handing over to them of a powerful army and air force by the British government on the dissolution of the Central African Federation in 1963. Furthermore, the settler government could be confident that it would survive the imposition of economic sanctions since not only did it have powerful friends in South Africa and the then Portuguese colonies of Angola and Mozambique, but the whole sanction exercise was full of loopholes.

Faced with this situation, Nkrumah made a further determined effort to bring the independent states of Africa 'to take the initiative in their own defence and that of the people of Zimbabwe'. The documents which follow show that on 19 November 1965 he:

a. requested the Secretary General of the OAU to convene a meeting of defence ministers and military chiefs of staff 'to plan ahead realistically to meet the danger which at the moment threatens Africa'
b. wrote to African heads of state proposing the signing of a Treaty of Mutual Defence and Security

Once again, Nkrumah's warnings of the dangers of delaying unified action on the part of the independent African states appeared to go unheeded except among the heads of the relatively few progressive states, which, like Nkrumah, regarded no part of Africa truly free while any part of the continent remained unliberated.

THREAT TO AFRICA

Nkrumah's press statement of 19 November 1965

I have called you here today to inform you that because of the growing gravity of the Southern Rhodesian crisis, I have requested the Secretary-General of the Organisation of African Unity to convene a meeting of defence ministers and their military chiefs of Staff so that the African states can plan ahead realistically to meet the danger which at the moment threatens Africa as a result of the Rhodesian rebellion.

The 200,000 racialist rebels in Southern Rhodesia are well provided with military resources. Both their army and air force are equipped and trained for warfare outside the frontiers of Southern Rhodesia. Indeed, the bulk of the air force could not be used for internal security purposes. Its only function is for external attack. The rebel Rhodesian Front Party is the Dominion Party of the former Federation re-named. The avowed object of this Party was to establish a 'White Dominion' consisting of Southern Rhodesia, parts of Zambia and Katanga, on the apartheid model of South Africa, and to link this with South Africa and the so-called Portuguese territory of Mozambique.

A rebel group in Southern Rhodesia with these declared objectives and in possession of a powerful army and air force is clearly a danger and a threat to the safety and security of the African states. The Security Council should therefore at once acknowledge that this rebellion is a threat to world peace and should act accordingly.

The present air force and armament of the Southern Rhodesia rebels were handed over to them by the United Kingdom government in 1963. Contrary to the resolution moved by Ghana and the warning which she sounded at the Security Council in an effort to prevent this dangerous and irresponsible act, the British government insisted on the transfer and vetoed the resolution of the Security Council. If this resolution had not been vetoed by Britain, it would have prevented the transfer of the army and airforce to the white minority settlers of Southern Rhodesia. Under these circumstances, it might be supposed that Britain would at least have immediately sent troops and aircraft to protect those African states which are now menaced by the very armed forces that two years ago Britain supplied to the Ian Smith regime.

Up till now nothing has been done militarily by the British government to quell the rebellion in Southern Rhodesia. I am convinced that it is dangerous for the independent African states to wait any longer for the United Kingdom to do its duty. The time has come for the independent African states to take the initiative in their own defence and that of the people of Zimbabwe.

Note from Nkrumah to heads of state of Congo, Zaire, Sudan, Uganda, Tanzania, Zambia, Guinea, 19 November 1965

Mr President and Dear Brother,

The illegal and unilateral declaration of independence by the minority settler government of Southern Rhodesia has flouted and shocked Africa and world opinion. Apart from declarations condemning the action of the Rhodesian settler regime, and the application of sanctions, it is clear that neither the United Kingdom government, nor the other world powers intend to take the necessary effective measures, including the use of force, to crush the Rhodesian rebellion.

The Rhodesian situation is a serious and direct threat to the peace of Africa, and unless the Organisation of African Unity can act quickly to meet the situation, the consequences to our continent will be incalculable.

As you know I have been advocating for a long time the establishment of an African High command which could resist such acts which threaten the territorial integrity and sovereignty of the African States. It was for this same reason that I proposed the creation of an Executive Council for the Organisation of African Unity.

The present situation therefore provides an urgent opportunity for us to mount an African force capable of being deployed against the illegal minority government of Southern Rhodesia.

The machinery of the Organisation of African Unity works

very slowly, and I am convinced that we must do something now to demonstrate that we are planning realistically to deal with the situation created by the racialist rebellion in Southern Rhodesia.

I suggest, in order to make our efforts more effective and realistic, that a Treaty of Mutual Defence and Security be signed between as many African states as possible, but beginning with:

> The Revolutionary Government of the Congo (Brazzaville)
> The Democratic Republic of the Congo (Leopoldville)
> Sudan
> Uganda
> Tanzania
> Zambia
> Guinea
> Ghana.

The object of this Treaty would be to deal with the possibility of hostilities breaking out between any of the states subscribing to the Treaty and Southern Rhodesia, Portugal and South Africa. Each member state of the Treaty shall pledge itself to go to the assistance of any country or countries subscribing to the Treaty. In other words an attack on any of these countries would be an attack on all of them. There would be no objection to other African countries adhering to this Treaty at any time they find it fit to do so.

If you are in favour of such a Treaty it is, I am sure, desirable that we formalise it as soon as possible. I suggest therefore that we should have a meeting in Accra attended by the defence ministers of those states which adhere to the Treaty to draw up the precise terms of the Treaty, and plan action. It will be valuable also if the meeting could be attended by the military advisers and chiefs of staff so that all technical points could be covered.

Please accept, Mr President, and dear Brother my fraternal sentiments.

8

CALL FOR ACTION IN RHODESIA

Speaking to the Ghana National Assembly on 25 November 1965, Nkrumah declared that Ghana had a duty to make constructive proposals to deal with the Rhodesian situation: 'If the UK rules out military intervention by its own forces and is opposed to military intervention by the UN or by the OAU, then the only way the Smith regime can be overthrown is by an internal revolt against the present illegal government.' He considered that Britain would not in fact be able to bring the Smith government down, and that it would be more appropriate for the UN to act by authorising African states, either collectively or individually, to intervene militarily to suppress the rebellion. If the African states intervened militarily, the UN should guarantee them against attack by Portugal or South Africa.

Nkrumah went on to announce the stopping of all military leave in Ghana and the formation of a voluntary militia, enrolment for which was to begin immediately. At the same time, he told members of the Assembly that they would be asked to enact legislation the following day, 26 November, to give the government power to prepare for any military eventuality. A Bill would give the government general powers to make all laws necessary for general mobilisation: 'A war against the rebels would not be like normal war,' he said, 'for every racialist in Southern Rhodesia there are sixteen Africans. Once arms have been put in their hands the war is as good as over. As I see it, if African forces are compelled to put down the Smith regime by force, this will be done not by conventional war but by organising a rising in mass by the people.' He went on to tell the

CALL FOR ACTION IN RHODESIA

Assembly that the Bill to be presented to them the following day would also give the government power to requisition Ghanaian aircraft and ships. It would not be possible for Ghana on its own to defeat the armed forces of the settler government. But if the Ghanaian forces were mobilised and properly deployed they could provide very powerful support for any African state threatened by the Smith regime.

Nkrumah's stand received enthusiastic support from Guinea. President Sékou Touré had already said in Nouakchott on 12 November 1965 that he regarded all African states as being in a state of war with Rhodesia. Guinea, he declared, was preparing an expeditionary force. But while other African states condemned UDI and imposed various trade, communications and diplomatic sanctions against Rhodesia, few were prepared to consider supporting Nkrumah and Sékou Touré in committing their countries to military intervention.

Nkrumah's address to the National Assembly, Accra, 25 November 1965

Exactly two weeks ago today, some European settlers in the British colony of Southern Rhodesia revolted against the government of the United Kingdom and seized control of the colonial machinery of government. It is now time that we took stock of the situation thus created and decided on what practical steps we should take.

Since then there have been directed against these settlers millions of words of denunciation. If words could kill, the entire rebel regime would be now in their graves. But rebellions are put down by action not by words. It is true there have been many calls for action but these have been calls for action by others. We must avoid the habit of looking outside the African continent to some former colonial power to set right those problems which are our duty to settle. The time has now come for us to take action ourselves. This means that we must examine the Southern Rhodesian rebellion with utmost realism and in the realities of the African revolution.

At first sight the rebellion in Southern Rhodesia appears to be aimed at enabling the settlers to continue unimpeded their policy of oppression and degradation of the African population. If we examine the circumstances of the revolt, however, it will be seen that this is not the explanation. The British government had already conceded to the settlers everything for which they asked short of formal independence. They could have continued as long as they liked to practise apartheid under the shadow of the Union Jack and with the assurance that whatever crime against humanity they committed they would be defended by the United Kingdom government at the United Nations.

Despite the fact that the present British government when in opposition had denounced the Southern Rhodesian constitution, despite the fact that the British prime minister had described Southern Rhodesia as a police state, the United Kingdom government were perfectly prepared to allow the settlers to continue to rule so long as they wished – provided only that they acknowledged the sovereignty of Britain. Why were they unwilling to do this? In such circumstances there can only be one reason for the rebellion, namely, that the settlers wished to demonstrate to the world that they were powerful enough to defy the might of Britain. Naturally they would not have embarked on this course unless previously they had obtained promises of support from South Africa and from Portugal. What we are facing is an alliance of the three apartheid countries aimed at taking over the whole of Southern Africa. The talk of Bechuanaland becoming independent in the near future becomes meaningless when viewed against this terrible background.

Let me first state the position of Ghana, which remains unchanged. We consider that the United Kingdom has under the charter of the United Nations certain positive obligations towards the African people of Southern Rhodesia which are set out in Article 73. If Britain is unwilling or unable to fulfil these obligations the United Nations must step in. Ghana considers that the proper organ through which the United Nations should intervene is the Organisation for African Unity. This view has now been supported by the Security Council of the United Nations.

In a resolution passed five days ago the Security Council

called on the United Kingdom – and I quote – *'to quell this rebellion of the racist minority and to take all other appropriate measures which would prove effective in eliminating the authority of the usurpers and in bringing the minority regime to an immediate end'*. Further, the resolution – and again I quote – *'called upon the Organisation of African Unity to do all in its power to assist in the implementation of this resolution in accordance with chapter 8 of the Charter'*. Chapter 8 provides that regional organisations such as the Organisation of African Unity may be empowered by the Security Council to take all suitable action, including military action.

In response to this decision of the Security Council, for which the United Kingdom government voted in favour, and in accordance with the resolution on Southern Rhodesia unanimously passed at the Assembly of Heads of State and Government of the Organisation of African Unity held in Accra last month, a Bill will be placed before you tomorrow, which will enable Ghana to play its full part in any action that may be decided upon.

I would remind you that in their resolution on Southern Rhodesia the Heads of State and Government decided that in the event of the failure of the United Kingdom government to take decisive action on the Southern Rhodesian issue, the African states would – and once again I quote – *'use all possible means, including the use of force, with a view to opposing a unilateral declaration of independence'*. In addition, the Heads of State and Government decided – and I quote once more – *'to give immediate and every necessary assistance to the people of Zimbabwe with a view to establishing a majority government in the country'*. The Bill which you will be asked to consider tomorrow will make it quite clear that Ghana is prepared to play its full part in implementing this resolution.

Ghana's position is that the United Kingdom government, having affirmed that it has full authority and responsibility for dealing with the Southern Rhodesian situation, should act to quell the rebellion. In my view, for the various reasons which I will explain later, it will prove impossible to quell the rebellion by purely economic means. From the very beginning of all this, I have made it clear to the British prime minister that I consider it would be necessary for Britain to use armed force against the rebels. I am still of this opinion. I am extremely doubtful as to whether sanctions could be operated effectively; and I can foresee that in the end it will be necessary either for the United Nations or the Organisation of African Unity to use military force to put down the rebellion, if the United Kingdom is unwilling to act.

I believe that it is possible, if a complete trade boycott were feasible, for the rebel regime to be overthrown in this way. Even so, nothing would be achieved by this except the creation of a state of anarchy, and unless there was an alternative government prepared and ready to take over from the rebels.

The British colony of Southern Rhodesia is a land-locked territory some one hundred and fifty thousand square miles in extent; in other words, it is about $1\frac{1}{2}$ times the size of Ghana. Southern Rhodesia is bounded on the north by Zambia and on the west by the British protectorate of Bechuanaland. It has a southern frontier with South Africa, and on the east a common frontier with Mozambique. Its rail communications are through Bechuanaland and through Portuguese territory. There is road but no rail communication direct with South Africa. An economic blockade of Southern Rhodesia would thus require the co-operation of four countries; the United Kingdom – which still controls the external relations of Bechuanaland, South Africa, Portugal and Zambia. Britain and Zambia are agreed on blockading Southern Rhodesia provided this is ordered by the United Nations. South Africa and Portugal have given no indication that they would accept a decision of the Security Council to impose economic sanctions. There is no economic reason why the United Kingdom should not enforce a blockade since Rhodesian trade with Britain represents less than one per cent of the United Kingdom total trade turnover. In contrast to this the sacrifice demanded of Zambia is colossal. One-third of Zambia's trade is with Southern Rhodesia. Further, all the essential imports required to keep the Zambian economy running are supplied through a railway system which passes through Southern Rhodesia.

If, therefore, as the United Kingdom government suggests,

the only method of bringing down the Smith regime is to be an economic blockade, this will impose on both Zambia and Malawi an intolerable economic burden, while the sacrifice made by Britain will be minimal. In any event if any economic blockade of Southern Rhodesia is to be effective, either the United Nations must compel Portugal and South Africa to join in economic sanctions or else all the other nations in the world must agree to extend sanctions so that they apply equally to the Portuguese colony of Mozambique and to South Africa. I hope that the United Nations would be prepared to take this action but I have doubts whether the Security Council, as at present composed, would vote in favour of this. If they are not prepared to do so, all talk of economic sanctions is nonsense.

It is possible, of course, in the coming elections to the Security Council for the African states to insist that only such states as are prepared to support a blockade of not only Southern Rhodesia but South Africa and Mozambique in addition, are elected to the Council. Even so, there is no guarantee that the United Nations Security Council has the authority to see that such a blockade was effectively enforced. For these reasons I believe that it will be extremely difficult, if not impossible, to defeat the Southern Rhodesian rebels by purely economic means.

If the United Kingdom government and the other major powers are sincere in their professed desire to carry out an effective blockade of Southern Rhodesia, the first step is clearly to inform Portugal and South Africa that United Nations inspectors will be sent to their territory to ensure that no goods are sent to Southern Rhodesia or are exported from it. If South Africa and Portugal refuse to accept this proposal then the Security Council must order that the same sanctions are applied against Mozambique and South Africa as are applied against Southern Rhodesia. The enforcing of such sanctions would result in, at least, a naval and air blockade of the whole of Southern Africa and would thus involve the use of far more military force than would be required if direct military action were taken against the Southern Rhodesian rebels. It is for this reason that I think the economic sanctions are unrealistic and that the only sensible course is for direct military action against the rebels. No one African state by itself can undertake this military action and if it were left to African states alone, they might well have to seek assistance from outside the African continent in order to deal with the situation, which might arise if Portugal or South Africa came militarily to the assistance of the rebels.

What then are we to do? Our first step must be to mobilise the conscience of the world so that in the last resort if African states are compelled to act on their own, they will have the sympathy of all peoples outside the African continent. At the moment far too little is known of the sordid history of Southern Rhodesia and the oppression suffered by its African inhabitants. We all have a duty to make the facts known.

A year ago when I was writing *Neocolonialism: The Last Stage of Imperialism*, I described the Southern Rhodesian situation, as it was then, in these words:

> 'Rhodesia, while theoretically a colony, is really a fossilised form of the earliest type of neocolonialism which was practised in Southern Africa until the formation of the Union of South Africa. The essence of the Rhodesia system is not to employ individuals drawn from the people of the territory itself to run the country, as in the newer type of neocolonial state, but to utilise instead an alien minority. The majority of the European ruling class of Rhodesia only came to the colony after the second world war, but it is they and not the African inhabitants, who outnumber them 16 to 1, that Britain regards as "the Government". This racialist state is protected from outside pressure because under international law it is a British colony, while Britain herself excuses her failure to exercise her legal rights to prevent the oppression and exploitation of the African inhabitants (of which, of course, she officially disapproves) because of a supposed British parliamentary convention. In other words, by maintaining Rhodesia nominally as a colony Britain in fact gives her official protection to a second South Africa and the European racialists are left free to treat the African inhabitants as they will.
>
> The Rhodesian system thus has all the hallmarks of the neocolonial model. The patron power, Britain, awards to a local government over which it claims to have no control unlimited rights and exploitation

within the territory. Yet Britain still retains powers to exclude other countries from intervening either to liberate its African population or to bring its economy into some other zone of influence. The manoeuvring over Rhodesia's "independence" is an excellent example of the workings of neocolonialism and of the practical difficulties to which the system gives rise. A European minority of less than a quarter of a million could not maintain, in the conditions of Africa today, rule over four million Africans without external support from somewhere. When the settlers talk of "independence" they are not thinking of standing on their own feet but merely of seeking a new neocolonialist master who would, in their view, be more reliable than Britain.'

That is what I wrote a year ago.

Southern Rhodesia came into existence by trickery and force of arms. At the close of the nineteenth century, Cecil Rhodes, the South African diamond buccaneer who had become prime minister of what was then the British dependency of Cape Colony, invaded Southern Rhodesia and Zambia. Rhodes, dreaming of the Cape to Cairo British empire, pushed from Matabeleland into Mashonaland across the Zambesi, into the country now called Zambia. Thus he drove a wedge between the Portuguese colonies of Mozambique and Angola. This expedition was undertaken by a pioneer column of mercenary free-booters who were recruited from among the English and Boer populations of South Africa. Each man who took part in the expedition was promised not less than fifteen gold claims and a farm of three thousand acres. These individuals were the first white settlers in Rhodesia and the National Day of Southern Rhodesia is described as 'Pioneer Day'.

It commemorates the arrival on the 12th of September, 1890, of this pioneer column at the spot where the present capital of Salisbury is now situated. Thus the first white settlers only arrived in Rhodesia and Zambia seventy-five years ago and they were a tiny minority among the African population. For the fifty years prior to the arrival of Rhodes' pioneer column, what is now Southern Rhodesia had been dominated by the Africans of Matabele. Their famous chief, Lo Bengula, was tricked into signing an agreement with Rhodes' agents under which he gave away to Rhodes' British South Africa Company all the mineral rights in his domain.

When Lo Bengula woke up to the bitter realisation of the trickery that had divested him and his people of the rights in their own land, he petitioned Queen Victoria. Despite the fact that Lo Bengula's letter showed clearly the nature of the fraud which had been perpetrated on him the British government of the day did nothing. Rhodes was allowed to bring in additional troops. He picked a quarrel with the Matabele, declared war on them and crushed them. The British government granted a charter to Rhodes' British South Africa Company which continued to rule Southern Rhodesia and Zambia up to 1923. In that year the British government organised a referendum among the white settlers of Southern Rhodesia so that they could decide whether they wished in future to join South Africa, or to be a *'self-governing British colony'*. The then population of some three million Africans were not allowed to vote and the only people participating in the plebiscite were some fourteen thousand European settlers. By a narrow majority they decided against joining South Africa.

In the same year the British government made a famous statement of policy known as 'The Devonshire Declaration' which is now reproduced in substance in Article 73 of the charter of the United Nations. The Devonshire Declaration declared, and I quote: *'His Majesty's government think it necessary definitely to record their considered opinion that the interests of the African natives must be paramount and if and when those interests and the interests of the immigrant races should conflict, the former should prevail.'* In the spirit of this declaration the British parliament insisted on maintaining some control at least over how the settlers treated the African majority of the colony. Since that date the whole history of Southern Rhodesia has consisted of the efforts made by the settlers to throw off this restraint and to obtain complete freedom to oppress and degrade the African population as they wished.

Their first attempt consisted of a plan to extend Southern Rhodesian settler control over what is now Zambia and Malawi. At first they had some success. In 1953, despite the opposition of the great majority of the African population of the territories concerned, the British government set up a federation composed of the colony of Southern Rhodesia and the then two British protectorates of Northern Rhodesia and Nyasaland. The constitution of this federation enacted by Britain, gave the political control of its government to the European settlers.

This federation lasted for only ten years. The heroic resistance of the peoples of Zambia and Malawi made it impossible for the European settlers to continue ruling and at the end of 1963 the federation was dissolved and Malawi and Zambia became independent. During the period of the federation's existence the present Rhodesian Front Party was born. It was called then the 'Dominion Party' because it had as its policy the creation of independent racial dominion which would include the rich copper belt areas of Zambia and Katanga as well as Southern Rhodesia. In 1962 this Dominion Party, re-christened the 'Rhodesian Front Party', won the settler general elections in Southern Rhodesia. They have ruled the colony ever since.

In a sense, the rebellion of Southern Rhodesia has been inevitable since September, 1963, when the British government frustrated a move by the Security Council of United Nations to prevent the arming of the Rhodesian settlers. What happened was this. During the time of the Federation of Rhodesia and Nyasaland the British Government built up a strong army and air force in the territory. In practice these forces were under the control of Britain though in name they belonged to the federation. When the federation broke up and its assets were being shared up neither Malawi nor Zambia was independent. And in any event these two states did not have the revenue or the facilities to keep hold of any but a very small part of the federation's air force and army. The British government proposed that the bulk of these armed forces should be handed over to the racist settlers of Southern Rhodesia.

As soon as it became known that Britain was intending to hand over the armed forces to the racist settlers, Ghana took the initiative of raising the question in the Security Council of the United Nations. This move was backed by all the African states. In the Security Council itself not only the African members,

Ghana and Morocco, but also all the other non-permanent members representing other regions of the world supported the Ghana resolution. Except for Britain, no single member of the Security Council was opposed to it. The resolution, moved by Ghana, would have prevented the handing over of any armed forces or military aircraft to the racist regime of Ian Smith. This regime was then already in power and had already boasted of its intention to seize independence by force. The resolution would have been carried and the subsequent revolt prevented except for the fact that the United Kingdom government used its veto to prevent it being passed.

Why did the United Kingdom government hand over these armed forces?

The United Kingdom government may have genuinely believed that by handing over these armies to Rhodesia, the settler government would be persuaded to accept the conditions demanded as a basis for the independence of Rhodesia and that an independent Rhodesia would act as a bulwark of Britain's east of Suez policy. This explains what is otherwise not clear about Britain's policy towards the rebellion in Rhodesia. The British quarrel with the settlers is that the Ian Smith regime has broken the implied bargain with Britain, and is now insisting on using Rhodesian armed forces for its own purpose. This purpose can only be one of aggression against other African states, in league with South Africa and Portugal. Under previous settler governments the condition of the African population was bad enough. Under the Rhodesian Front Party it became intolerable. Indeed the persecution of the African population of Southern Rhodesia has reached such a pitch that the continuation of settler rule in any form is impossible.

Just before the rebellion began, three recently recruited Southern Rhodesian policemen from Britain deserted, horrified at the conditions in Rhodesia. Now back in Britain they have been telling British newspapers of their experiences. They say they were told by the settler officers to shoot Africans to kill and thus save hospital fees. They were advised not to hit Africans on the head, '*as it's four times thicker than a European's*', but to '*remember that the African has a weak stomach*' – and aim for that. They claim that the police deliberately incite African riots. Nor are they the only witnesses to the callous brutality with which the four million African population is treated. The Roman Catholic Archbishop and Bishops of Southern Rhodesia have declared and I quote from their pastoral letter: *'Wages are inadequate, housing conditions in many instances are unworthy of human beings, and terms of employment are such that husbands are separated for long periods from their wives. Such a state of affairs cries to heaven for vengeance and even in the natural order can only breed crime and chaos.'*

Under the Land Apportionment Act passed by the settler government all the best land is given to the Europeans. Four million Africans are compelled to live on the worse land while the 217,000 Europeans occupy one-half of the total farming area. The treatment of African domestic servants, of whom there are some 80,000 is little short of slavery. There are no schools for their children. Husbands and wives are not allowed to live together or have their children with them. A servant cannot see a film, go to a dance, attend an athletic event, hear a lecture or go for a walk at night. If he stays at home and drinks an alcoholic beverage he is guilty of a criminal offence for which he can be punished by a term of imprisonment. Similar conditions apply to most of the industrial workers. They are compelled to live in African 'locations' where, as often as not, they are separated from their families. Eighty per cent of the accommodation provided for the African workers of Salisbury is for single men. Usually four men are compelled to live and cook in one small room. The African town worker may only have a visitor to stay with him if he obtains the permission of a superintendent of a location; he may only leave his lodging for two weeks unless he obtains special permission; and in many cases may not be out of doors after 9 p.m. He automatically loses his home if he is dismissed by his employer or if he is convicted of any political offence or even if he transgresses some of the provisions of the 'Pass' Laws.

Against these conditions the African population of Southern Rhodesia has sought to establish political parties which could organise opposition to oppression. The Zimbabwe African Peoples Union – ZAPU – was established after the African

People's Conference in Accra in 1958 and campaigned against the efforts of the settlers to negotiate with the British government a constitution which would give the settlers a freer hand than they had already possessed for ill-treating and oppressing the bulk of the population. In spite of the opposition of ZAPU, Britain insisted on granting to the settlers the notorious 1961 constitution. This constitution was at the time denounced in the British parliament by the British Labour Party, then in opposition. It was condemned by an overwhelming majority of the General Assembly in the United Nations which asked Britain not to bring it into force. Nevertheless the constitution was established and it has subsequently provided the means by which Ian Smith has established his illegal regime.

Ghana believes, as I think do all other African states, that it is a tragic misfortune that ZAPU has now been split and that there are in Southern Rhodesia two nationalist African parties, each claiming to speak for the African people. Nevertheless such disunity is bound to occur in conditions where all political activity is forbidden, the leaders of both parties are imprisoned, and there is no opportunity to test by free elections which party the people support. At all costs we must avoid a situation in which we refuse to support the masses of the African people of Southern Rhodesia merely on the ground that two parties are claiming their allegiance. A simple election on a universal franchise could easily decide this.

It is clear that the African people of Southern Rhodesia are today putting up a strong resistance to the illegal Smith regime and they deserve our full support. There is nothing now to be gained by recrimination over past events. The United Kingdom government has stated it is determined to end the rebellion and to establish a new regime in Southern Rhodesia. As a member of the United Nations of the Organisation of African Unity and of the Commonwealth, Ghana has a duty to make positive and constructive proposals to Britain as to how this may be done. The problem can be looked at under two heads. First, how is the rebellion to be ended? And, secondly, when the rebellion is over what type of government is to be substituted for the present regime? These two questions are closely interrelated. If the United

CALL FOR ACTION IN RHODESIA

Kingdom rules out military intervention by its own forces and is opposed to military intervention by the United Nations or by the Organisation of African Unity, then the only way the Smith regime can be overthrown is by an internal revolt against the present illegal government. But such an internal revolt can only be brought about if those seeking to restore law and order within Southern Rhodesia are given positive assurances as to what will happen to them after they have overthrown Smith. No single person in Southern Rhodesia is prepared to move a finger to restore the discredited 1961 constitution. Therefore, it seems clear that if the United Kingdom government really wants to create an effective opposition to Smith within Southern Rhodesia, it must not only revoke the 1961 constitution forthwith but also hold out hopes for something better in the future.

Up till now, according to the United Kingdom government, the one obstacle to holding a Southern Rhodesia constitutional conference at which all political parties would be represented, was that Smith's settler government was opposed to the holding of such a conference and the British government could not override his wishes. Well, the Smith government is no more. From Britain's point of view, Smith and his cabinet are private citizens and what they say or do has no constitutional validity. In any event, if Smith had continued as the legal prime minister of Southern Rhodesia, the British government were pledged to considering the holding of a constitutional conference despite his opposition. I will quote to you the exact words of this pledge as set out in the final communique of the last Commonwealth Prime Minister's Conference:

> *'In this process of seeking to reach agreement on Rhodesia's advance to independence a constitutional conference would, at the appropriate time, be a natural step. If the discussions did not develop satisfactorily in this direction in a reasonably speedy time, the British government having regard to the principle enunciated by the Commonwealth Secretary of unimpeded progress towards majority rule would be ready to consider promoting such a conference in order to ensure Rhodesia's progress to independence on a basis acceptable to the people of Rhodesia as a whole.'*

What should be the theme of this constitutional conference? Again, I quote from the same communique, which states that the other Commonwealth Heads of Government *'welcomed the statement of the British government that the principle of "one man one vote" was regarded as the very basis of democracy and this should be applied to Rhodesia'*.

In my view the United Kingdom government should summon immediately a constitutional conference to devise a constitution for Southern Rhodesia which would provide for the establishment of majority rule in the shortest practical time. The United Kingdom government should state that once majority rule had been established on a firm basis, Zimbabwe should become independent, but that there should be no question of Southern Rhodesia becoming independent on any other basis than 'one man one vote'. But we must be realistic. The downfall of the Smith regime will create a vacuum. This vacuum must immediately be filled by the United Kingdom. Britain must establish immediately a system of direct rule through agencies immediately responsible to the British government so that conditions can be created for the emergence of a constitutional government based on universal adult suffrage.

If the people of Southern Rhodesia are to rise against Smith without any external military aid, they have a hard and desperate task before them. They cannot be expected to undertake that task unless they have a clear goal before them. A constitutional conference now is the first requirement of the situation.

There is only one basic problem in Southern Rhodesia. It is the presence of the white settlers. It is therefore Britain's duty to consider means by which those of them who will not co-operate with a majority government can be induced to leave. It is quite wrong to suppose that the majority of these settlers are people who have lived in Southern Rhodesia for generations. The majority of them came there after the last world war to escape the austerity and high taxation which had to be faced in Britain as a result of Britain's part in the struggle against Hitler. Clifford Dupont, the so-called officer administering the rebel government, is still enrolled as a solicitor in London. He only left England in 1948 and it would be no hardship to him if he

CALL FOR ACTION IN RHODESIA

was compelled to resume his British law practice. The majority of Rhodesian Front supporters are similarly situated. At the time of Indonesian independence, the Netherlands, which is a small country and heavily populated, nevertheless repatriated to Holland over two hundred thousand colonial residents of the former East Indian colonies.

I propose that discussions should take place immediately among Commonwealth governments to see how many settlers could be resettled in other Commonwealth countries. At the moment, Australia, for example, is calling out for European immigrants. Grants and assisted passages are provided by Australia for tens of thousands of settlers from Austria, Germany and other European countries. The older Commonwealth countries could, I believe, make a positive contribution by agreeing to take a fixed quota of such Southern Rhodesian settlers as wished to leave.

Short of these major measures, there are certain other positive steps which Britain could take here and now. The United Kingdom government has now taken power to legislate for Southern Rhodesia and it has used this power to declare illegal the Press censorship imposed by Smith. Britain should, I consider, immediately use these same powers to revoke all the detention orders in force against African nationalists who have been imprisoned for opposing the Smith regime. How can Britain possibly hope that Smith will be overthrown and British authority reasserted if the United Kingdom government do nothing to aid those who have been imprisoned for opposing the rebels? It seems to me extraordinary that even in the case of Mr Garfield Todd, who was a missionary from New Zealand and was for five years prime minister of Southern Rhodesia, nothing has been done by the British government to free him from detention.

Finally, there is the question of the armed forces and the police. Almost all the European officers in the police are British, as are about one-third of the officers in the army and air force. Southern Rhodesian citizens only comprise a small fraction of the Rhodesian armed forces and police and, next to Britain, South Africa provides the largest contingent. Without their

British officers, the Southern Rhodesian air force, army and police would be crippled. It seems to me imperative that Britain should recall at once all British air force and police officers and should state that the United Kingdom government would regard as treason the action of any British subject who continued to serve in the Smith forces after a certain date. Many of these officers are in receipt of pensions from Britain for past services in the United Kingdom police or defence forces. It should be made clear that the pensions of any officers who continue to serve under Smith will be forfeited.

If the United Kingdom government were to take the various steps which I have outlined, it is possible that these would bring the rebels down but there is no certainty of this. It is therefore much more appropriate that the Southern Rhodesian question is dealt with by the United Nations. Hitherto the United Kingdom government has always claimed that Southern Rhodesia is a purely internal matter. Such a claim is nonsense today. British authority does not extend beyond a deserted villa in the suburbs of Salisbury where the British governor wanders through the empty corridors.

The Resolution of the Security Council taken five days ago states – and I quote its actual words: '*That the situation resulting from the proclamation of independence by the illegal authorities in Southern Rhodesia is extremely serious, that the United Kingdom government should put an end to it and that its continuance in time constitutes a threat to international peace and security.*'

It is important to note that this wording places the Southern Rhodesia issue under Chapter 7 of the charter of the United Nations which is the chapter that deals with threats to world peace and which enables the Security Council to give mandatory instructions to all member states. Under this chapter the United Nations can halt all road, rail and air communication with Southern Rhodesia. It can also order military sanctions. I consider that the Security Council must, if the United Nations is to survive as an effective force, order such military sanctions if the present economic sanctions are proved ineffective against the Rhodesian rebellion.

It is necessary to point out that the Security Council can

CALL FOR ACTION IN RHODESIA

order military intervention without necessarily setting up a United Nation's force. In my view it would be much better if the Security Council of the United Nations were to authorise African states, either collectively or individually, to intervene militarily to suppress the rebellion in Southern Rhodesia in the event of the United Kingdom government being unable or unwilling to do so. It would be desirable if all permanent members of the Security Council guaranteed against attack by Portugal or South Africa the African states undertaking these police measures on behalf of the United Nations. But it would not be necessary in practice for all the permanent members to give such a guaranteee. If it could be obtained from one of them it would be sufficient.

Finally, it is necessary to consider the possible role of the Organisation of African Unity. It could, of course, act in concert with the United Kingdom government if the members were convinced that Britain genuinely intended to put down the revolt. The Zambian government has already offered the United Kingdom military bases in Zambia if Britain desires to place forces in Africa either to suppress the rebellion or at least to protect those African states which are threatened by the rebels. The United Kingdom has not accepted Zambia's generous offer. Nevertheless, in order to make Ghana's position clear, I wish to state that if the British government desires to use Ghanaian territory for any purpose connected with the suppression of the Southern Rhodesian government we shall accord every facility possible.

The second possible role which the Organisation of African Unity might undertake is to act as a peace force of the United Nations. For this purpose it is essential that we establish a unified military command and engage as soon as possible in detailed planning so that we deploy our military forces to the best advantage.

Finally, the Organisation of African Unity must consider what action it will take if both Britain and the United Nations fail within a given time effectively to deal with the Southern Rhodesian situation. If a cry for help comes to us from the victims of oppression in Southern Rhodesia, we, the African states, must answer it. It is for this reason that the National Assembly is being asked tomorrow to enact legislation to give the government power to prepare for any military eventuality. The Bill which will be introduced under a certificate of urgency seeks to give the government general powers to make all laws necessary for mobilisation. Already the first steps in this direction have been taken. Members of the armed forces who have completed their time of service are being retained in the forces. As a precaution all military leave has been stopped.

Under existing law we are going to establish a militia. This militia will be a voluntary force. Its members will not be paid. Their training will be on a part-time basis and their enrolment is to start on Monday next.

Under the Bill which you will be asked to pass the government is given power to requisition Ghanaian aircraft and ships. You may remember that at the time of the Congo crisis the western powers failed to provide us with the air transport which they had promised. The government cancelled all internal and external services of Ghana Airways and used the aircraft to transport our troops. We shall not hesitate to do the same thing again. The Bill also enables airports, seaports and roads to be closed in whole or in part in order to facilitate troop movements. I must warn you that a mobilisation on the scale which we have in mind must entail considerable disorganisation of civilian life but in a crisis of this nature we must put military necessity first.

In everything we must be realistic; it would not be possible for Ghana alone to defeat the forces of the Southern Rhodesian settlers. Nevertheless Ghana forces, if properly mobilised and deployed, could provide very powerful support for any African state which was threatened by the Smith regime. Ghana, in conjunction with a number of other African states who may have taken the same steps of military preparedness as we have done, would certainly be able to defeat the rebels.

Any war against the rebels would not be like a normal war. For every racialist in Southern Rhodesia there are sixteen Africans. Once arms have been put in their hands the war is as good as over. As I see it, if African armed forces are compelled to put down the Smith regime by force then this will not be done

CALL FOR ACTION IN RHODESIA

by means of conventional warfare but by organising a rising in mass by the people.

I consider that when the African states meet at Addis Ababa on the 3rd December, there is one other step which should be considered most seriously. Outside the African continent there are thousands — indeed hundreds of thousands — of individuals with military training who are prepared to fight against racialism. In fact I have already received numerous telegrams and letters from individuals and organisations outside Africa who are prepared to fight for the liberation of Zimbabwe. We must consider realistically how we can mobilise and equip them. In some countries voluntary contributions could be organised by which these volunteers would be provided with the necessary equipment. This is a proposal we must consider in all its implications. In any event it is my firm view that at the forthcoming Addis Ababa meeting the African Defence Organisation, which was approved by the Heads of State at the recent Accra Summit Conference, should be set up immediately.

It is unfortunate that the proposal which I made two years ago for the setting up of an African High Command was not taken up, otherwise Africa would not find itself in this predicament.

These are serious days for the world. I wish that I could believe that the United Kingdom government was sincere in its desire to put down the rebellion but from its past actions I see no sign of it. I hope that time may prove me wrong. If it does not, then a heavy responsibility will fall upon all African states and we in Ghana must today begin to prepare to take our share in that responsibility.

9

GHANA BREAKS DIPLOMATIC RELATIONS WITH BRITAIN

Nkrumah set a time limit for Britain to end the settler rebellion in Rhodesia. When the time limit expired on 15 December 1965, Ghana in compliance with the OAU resolution agreed at the 1965 Accra Summit meeting, broke off diplomatic relations with Britain. A note was delivered to Harold Wilson informing him of the decision and stating: 'In the opinion of the government of Ghana a severance of diplomatic relations with Britain would mean Ghana's withdrawal from the Commonwealth.'

In delivering the message, the Ghanaian Minister of Trade, formerly High Commissioner in London, apparently emphasised that no date had been set. As the note from Wilson to Nkrumah dated 15 December shows, Wilson got the clear impression from the Ghanaian Minister of Trade that 'Ghana would give us time for manoeuvre and reasonable time to bring Mr Smith's rebellion to an end'.

Apart from it being out of character for Nkrumah to make empty threats or to go against a resolution of the OAU, Ghana did in fact sever diplomatic relations with Britain on 15 December 1965. On the following day, 16 December, Nkrumah addressed the National Assembly in Accra and told them officially that: 'The government of Ghana has severed diplomatic relations with Britain as from yesterday, and the United Kingdom government has been informed accordingly.'

No firm date was set for withdrawal from the Commonwealth because, as the documents in this section show, Nkrumah was engaged in trying to

GHANA BREAKS DIPLOMATIC RELATIONS

get other African states to withdraw at the same time. In his Address to the National Assembly in Accra on 16 December 1965, Nkrumah announced that Ghana proposed to 'place before the next OAU Summit conference a resolution calling on all member states of the OAU to sever such links as stand in the way of African unity or impede its progress, whether such links be with the French, British, Spanish, Portuguese, Belgians, or what have you'. Nkrumah had for a long time held that membership of the Commonwealth and the French Community, having their roots in Africa's colonial past, would end with the formation of a viable political union of African states.

In all, only nine African states, of which two – Ghana and Tanzania – are Commonwealth members, complied with the OAU resolution and broke off diplomatic relations with Britain in protest against her refusal to use military means to end the settler rebellion.

Letter from Nkrumah to Harold Wilson, 11 December, 1965

My dear Prime Minister,

As you know, Ghana has participated actively as a member of the Commonwealth and had even proposed the establishment of a Secretariat in order to make the Commonwealth more in tune with the common aspirations of its members. However, Ghana's continued membership of the Commonwealth has been misunderstood and is being exploited in an attempt to set up rival blocs in Africa which if not checked could defeat the objectives of African unity. Ghana's membership within the Commonwealth has made it difficult for her to pursue boldly and effectively her African objectives, namely, the struggle against colonialism and neocolonialism and the establishment of an All-African Union Government.

This dilemma has been heightened by the present crisis in Southern Rhodesia and by the inadequate manner in which Britain has so far handled the rebellion. In this connection, the Organisation of African Unity has decided that if by the 15th of December, 1965, Britain has not taken any positive and effective action to crush the rebellion in Southern Rhodesia, then member states should sever diplomatic relations with the United Kingdom.

Britain has not as yet solved the Southern Rhodesian problem. Ghana's position is that sanctions alone are not adequate unless they are backed by Britain's military intervention. Since, so far, there has not been any military action by Britain to quell the rebellion, I foresee no immediate end of the Ian Smith regime.

I have, therefore, after long and deep reflection and serious consideration, decided to comply with the OAU resolution. The government of Ghana has accordingly decided to break off diplomatic relations with Britain as soon as possible after the 15th December, 1965, if there is no end to the Ian Smith regime by that date. In the opinion of the government of Ghana a severance of diplomatic relations with Britain would mean Ghana's withdrawal from the Commonwealth.

I am therefore sending you a delegation led by Mr Kwesi Armah, Minister of Trade, and former High Commissioner in London, to inform you of my decision in this matter. In due course I shall take the opportunity of informing Her Majesty the Queen of Ghana's decision to leave the Commonwealth.

Message from Wilson to Nkrumah, 15 December 1965

Kwesi Armah called on me yesterday to deliver your letter of 11 December, for which very many thanks. We had a long discussion in the course of which Kwesi Armah emphasised that the words 'as soon as possible' in the fourth paragraph of your letter were to be taken to mean that you were not contemplating breaking off diplomatic relations with us or taking other similar action in the immediate future. He emphasised that you understood the difficulties of our position and wished to interpret the resolution passed at the OAU meeting in Addis Ababa last week in a manner which would give us room for manoeuvre and reasonable time to bring Mr Smith's rebellion to an end. Kwesi Armah went on to say that if the British government did not succeed 'as soon as possible' then you would break off diplomatic relations with us and also leave the Commonwealth.

I explained our position at length to Kwesi Armah. I also

GHANA BREAKS DIPLOMATIC RELATIONS

had a long discussion with Abubakar last night about his proposal for a special meeting of Commonwealth Heads of Government in Africa early next month and told him that I would be very ready to play my part in it. I would therefore urge you at least to wait for this before taking any irrevocable decisions. Meanwhile the whole matter has now been transferred to the Security Council where we have indicated that we are prepared to take a thoroughly constructive attitude.

Note from Nkrumah to Sékou Touré, 15 December 1965

My dear Brother and Colleague,

In compliance with the recent OAU resolution on Southern Rhodesia, Ghana has informed Britain of her intention to withdraw from the Commonwealth and break off diplomatic relations with Britain if by the 15th of December Britain has not taken positive steps to crush the rebellion.

I am, therefore, sending you Mr A. K. Puplampu, Minister of Lands, as special envoy, to apprise you of my decision.

Please accept, my dear Brother and Colleague, the assurance of my highest consideration.

Nkrumah's address to the National Assembly, Accra, 16 December 1965

The House will recall that at the Summit Conference of the Organisation of African Unity held at Accra last October, it was unanimously decided that in the event of the failure on the part of the United Kingdom to use all possible means, including the use of force, to oppose a unilateral declaration of independence by the Southern Rhodesian settlers, all members of the Organisation of African Unity would reconsider, among other matters, their diplomatic relations with the United Kingdom. In accordance with this resolution, when it became clear that the United Kingdom government was not using effective means to quell the rebellion, the Council of Ministers meeting recently at Addis Ababa unanimously decided that all member states of the Organisation of African Unity should break off diplomatic relations with Britain. The decision was that if by the 15th of December, that is yesterday, Britain had not put down the rebellion, we of the independent African states should sever diplomatic relations with Britain.

The breaking of diplomatic relations is a serious step, and the Ghana government had therefore hoped that the United Kingdom government would take some action which might justify African States refraining from making a move which, however valuable as a protest, must have grave consequences.

Since 1963, I have continuously emphasised to the British government the seriousness of the situation in Southern Rhodesia and the dangers it could pose for our relationship, unless it were handled firmly and effectively. In particular, I pointed out the serious consequences inherent in the transfer of the attributes of sovereignty to Rhodesia without majority rule. I have also stressed time and again that the handing over of the armed forces which the British had built up for the former Central African Federation to a minority settler regime whose avowed policy has always been to maintain a racialist state was bound to lead to a situation such as confronts us today. It is against this background that Ghana raised this question at the Security Council in September, 1963, and urged the Council to call upon the United Kingdom government not to hand over these armed forces and other attributes of sovereignty to the Southern Rhodesian minority settler regime. As you know, all my warnings went unheeded, and my forebodings have come true. Indeed, by vetoing Ghana's resolution the United Kingdom government actually made the present situation inevitable. History thus holds Britain responsible.

It is therefore clear that my government has taken all possible steps to let the British government know of Africa's concern in an effort to avoid the present crisis. We have consistently urged on the United Kingdom government policies which could have averted the present unhappy situation. Only last Tuesday, I sent a special delegation to deliver a personal message from me to the prime minister of the United Kingdom, Mr Harold Wilson. In that message I made it clear to the British prime minister that as there was no evidence that Britain was taking positive and effective action to quell the rebellion in Southern Rhodesia, the government of Ghana was in honour bound to carry out the decision taken by the Organisation of African Unity at Addis Ababa on the 3rd December this year.

I have considered very carefully a reply which Mr Wilson sent to me yesterday. There is nothing in Mr Wilson's letter which could justify a change in our position. Ghana's position is that sanctions alone are inadequate, unless backed by military intervention. I am still of the view that the measures which Britain proposes to take are inadequate to deal with the situation. The United Kingdom government shows no intention of taking military action to quell this rebellion.

The government of Ghana has, therefore, severed diplomatic relations with Britain as from yesterday, and the United Kingdom government has been informed accordingly.

I would like to make it clear that the rupture of relations with Britain does not affect British business interests or individuals in Ghana, nor does it affect the services of British technical and professional personnel (including those in the armed forces) recruited directly by the Ghana government or on loan to us through technical assistance from the United Kingdom.

If and when the United Kingdom government succeeds in crushing the Ian Smith rebellion and solves the Rhodesian crisis in the interests of the majority of the Rhodesian people, the government of Ghana will normalize relations

It would appear that British policy in regard to Southern Rhodesia is to treat what is essentially an African problem as though it were exclusively a British concern. Up to the very last moment I was hoping that the United Kingdom government would show some response to the initiative of the Organisation of African Unity. In all this, the British prime minister has gone to the utmost lengths to make every concession to the Ian Smith regime. Throughout, Mr Wilson has disregarded the feelings of the African people in this matter. In this connection, it is futile to talk of further Commonwealth prime ministers' meetings at this time, when the undertakings given by the British government at the last Prime Ministers' Conference in London have been totally ignored.

RHODESIA FILE

The Southern Rhodesian issue has brought to a head a more fundamental question affecting the interests and destiny of Africa. Upon this issue all African states must take a definite stand. I would like to clarify this point further. By the accident of history almost all the independent African states were once colonies of European powers and because of this the relationships and associations formed during the colonial period have continued in one form or another even after independence. Typical of such associations is the French Community or the British Commonwealth, to which Ghana chose to belong of her own free will after independence.

On the other hand, our policy in Africa has been based on the fundamental necessity to establish an all-African approach to the problems of the African continent. This is why I have been advocating the establishment of a continental union Government of Africa all these years.

The movement for African unity has now made considerable progress and will continue to grow until it reaches its goal: a union government for all Africa. It is clear, however, that the Commonwealth connection is misunderstood by the non-Commonwealth countries in Africa and is used by them as an argument for setting up other groupings which seek to foster active links with former colonial powers.

As you know, Ghana has participated actively as a member of the Commonwealth and had even proposed the establishment of a Commonwealth Secretariat in order to make the Commonwealth more in tune with the common aspirations of its members. However, Ghana's membership within the Commonwealth has made it difficult for her to pursue boldly and effectively her African objectives, namely the struggle against colonialism and neocolonialism and the establishment of an All-African Union Government. This difficulty has been highlighted by the present crisis in Southern Rhodesia and by the inadequate manner in which the United Kingdom government has so far handled the rebellion.

The conception of the Commonwealth was built upon the idea that it provided a bridge between peoples of all races and of all stages of development. The manner in which events in

GHANA BREAKS DIPLOMATIC RELATIONS

Southern Rhodesia have been handled by the United Kingdom Government has undermined and betrayed this conception.

In these circumstances, and in order to preserve African unity so as to facilitate the earliest formation of a Union Government for Africa, the government of Ghana must consider withdrawing from the Commonwealth. To this end, we propose to hold the necessary consultations within the Organisation of African Unity as to the severance from ex-colonial powers of ties which militate against African unity.

As I said before, African unity and our endeavours to establish a Union Government for Africa are imperilled by African states forming links with their ex-colonial masters. Our unity can only be preserved and a union government achieved and stabilised if we sever links with former colonial powers whose continuing interest in our continent only breeds disunity among us.

For this reason, the government of Ghana will place before the next Organisation of African Unity Summit Conference a resolution calling upon all member states of the Organisation of African Unity to sever such links as stand in the way of African unity or impede its progress, whether such links be with the French, British, Spanish, Portuguese, Belgian or what have you. Such united action by all members states of the Organisation of African Unity is the best means and the surest way of guaranteeing the unity and security of the independent states of Africa.

I have taken this opportunity to make Ghana's position clear to the world and in particular to our brothers and colleagues of our sister states of Africa. It is my view that, in the interest of African unity, there should be no political or economic regrouping or blocs in Africa in alliance with an ex-colonial power or any foreign power for that matter. And any economic grouping in Africa must be only under the aegis and umbrella of the Organisation of African Unity.

In pursuit of this objective the time has now come for the Organisation of African Unity to create and develop the essential machinery for African unity, namely:

a. a Common Monetary Authority which will enable us to

pool our resources in order to survive the pressures which can be applied to us
b. an All-African Common Market to serve our expanding economies
c. an African High Command which can defend our continent and ensure the security of the member states, and
d. an Executive to co-ordinate and harmonise our efforts on an all-African basis.

The Southern Rhodesian crisis has once again exposed the weakness of the Organisation of African Unity. If, as I had proposed at the Accra Summit Conference, an Executive of the Organisation of African Unity had been established, we would now have been fully prepared to carry out the decisions of the Accra Summit Conference and the Addis Ababa meeting of the Council of Ministers in regard to the Rhodesian crisis. If we had had an African High Command we would now be in a better position to give military assistance to our brothers in Zambia and Zimbabwe. As I have said before, military operations are a complex and difficult matter. They cannot be suddenly improvised. If we blame Britain for not having taken steps in advance to deal with the Southern Rhodesian rebels, the African states must equally blame themselves for not having made adequate preparations to deal with such situations.

Today Africa is facing a great challenge – in fact the greatest challenge in its chequered history. And we must act in such a way as to uphold her honour and dignity. Let no one underrate or miscalculate the strength of a united Africa.

10

THE INADEQUACY OF ECONOMIC SANCTIONS

By January 1966, a large number of countries had complied with UN and OAU resolutions calling for a complete economic embargo on Rhodesia. Details of the economic sanctions to be applied by member states of the OAU were contained in the final communique of the Council of Ministers issued from Addis Ababa on 5 December 1965. Among the decisions announced was a total blockade of Rhodesia; the suspension of all economic relations and the freezing of Rhodesian accounts in African banks; the suppression of all transport systems to and from Rhodesia, including the right of overflying aircraft, and a ban on cable, telephone, telex and radio-telephone links with Rhodesia.

Britain's lead in imposing oil sanctions on 17 December 1965, had been followed by other oil exporting countries, with the notable exception of the United States, which for legal reasons could only issue a directive to oil companies advising them not to supply Rhodesia.

The imposition of sanctions meant that officially about 54 per cent of Rhodesia's exports were under boycott. If the oil boycott was totally effective, it was estimated that Rhodesia would run out of oil supplies in about eight to ten weeks. But supplies might stretch to six months if rationing was introduced. Those who wished to believe in the effectiveness of sanctions, further estimated that if no successful counter-measures were taken by Rhodesia there would be a fall in the national income of approximately 21 per cent by the end of the first year of the boycott. As far as Rhodesia's vital tobacco trade was concerned, it was reckoned that sanctions would bring it to a virtual standstill. In 1964, Rhodesia's total exports of tobacco amounted to £41 million. Countries which declared an embargo on Rhodesian tobacco imports by mid-December 1965, imported £30,252,000 worth of tobacco in 1964.

However, it remained to be seen how effectively the trade and communications sanctions against the settler government would be applied. Much would depend on (1) the sincerity of those who declared them, and the extent to which they would be able, or willing to ensure that the sanctions were strictly observed, and (2) the effectiveness of the Rhodesian government's counter-measures.

The Smith government had plenty of time before UDI to consider very carefully the possible effects of an economic blockade. On 26 April 1965, a Rhodesian government White Paper dealt with this specific question, and gave a detailed analysis of how sanctions would affect the Rhodesian economy. It was explained that 'Rhodesia would obtain elsewhere all those imports which today it gets from Britain and the Commonwealth, and that a great proportion of the country's exports could be marketed in those countries with whom Rhodesia has trading relations.' The White Paper concluded that the Rhodesian government was quite satisfied that for economic sanctions to be effective, concerted action by all the trading nations of the world would be necessary, and that this was very unlikely to occur. Rhodesians, therefore, had 'nothing to lose but all to gain by accepting their responsibilities and becoming completely independent as a sovereign state'.

As far as oil sanctions were concerned – to give one example only – the pipeline from Beira to Umtali was alone handling 600,000 tons a year, and the Belgian oil company, Petrofina, which had a large shareholding in Petrangol, the Portuguese company operating in Angola, let it be known that if Portugal wanted supplies to be sent to Rhodesia, Petrangol would be obliged to comply. Before UDI, Rhodesia made a deal to obtain oil through a Portuguese oil company, Sonau, and its subsidiary Sonarep, which had oilfields in Angola. Further arrangements were made with the French oil company, Total, which had a subsidiary in South Africa.

Other sanction-breaking arrangements and operations covering all areas of trade to and from Rhodesia are too numerous to mention. At that time, the 'white triangle' of Portugal, Rhodesia and South Africa was still virtually intact in central and southern Africa, and both open and

THE INADEQUACY OF ECONOMIC SANCTIONS

secret arrangements could be made to ensure the continuance of the minority government in Rhodesia. For example, within ten days after UDI the South African Rembrandt Tobacco Corporation revealed an offer to buy the whole Rhodesian tobacco crop for 1966. Rhodesian tobacco farmers, having sold the entire 1965 crop before UDI, then proceeded to plant for 1966 with a 5 per cent increase in acreage to make up for the loss of preference in the British market. There could hardly have been a more confident display of contempt for the efforts of those imposing sanctions.

It was not surprising, therefore, that the Smith government felt secure. Smith himself described the imposition of sanctions as 'a nine day wonder', and forecast that they would gradually disappear leaving the white settlers in control. His confidence proved not ill-founded. As the weeks and months passed after UDI it became apparent that while sanctions might damage the Rhodesian economy, they would be insufficient to topple the government. It was abundantly clear that Rhodesians could obtain any imports they could afford to buy. All necessary goods could be purchased through South Africa or the then Portuguese territories of Angola and Mozambique.

Nkrumah had never been in any doubt about the inadequacy of economic sanctions, and he regarded Wilson's boast that sanctions would end the settler rebellion 'in weeks rather than months' as hypocrisy.

The British government had declared even before UDI that it was not prepared to use force to quell the rebellion. The UN and the OAU, while passing strong resolutions, seemed equally unwilling to embark on military action. Therefore, there only remained the possibility of African states organising a forceful overthrow of the settler regime, preferably with the blessing of the UN. If such a force could be organised it would have the advantage of being able to act in the closest co-operation with the liberation movement already active within Rhodesia. This was one of the main purposes of Nkrumah's initiative when he proposed a Treaty of Mutual Defence and Security and the formation of an All-African High Command. For as Nkrumah pointed out in the government statement of 10 January 1966, the key to a solution to the Rhodesian problem lay not in simply bringing down the Smith government but in establishing majority rule: 'Settler rule, in the view of the government of Ghana, stands condemned and cannot be allowed to continue in any form whatsoever.'

Ghana government statement of 10 January 1966

The government of Ghana considers it desirable in view of various discussions taking place on the Southern Rhodesian situation to restate its position.

The Ghana government believes that the present economic sanctions, as advocated by the United Kingdom government, are quite inadequate to deal with the situation. Even if these sanctions were successful in bringing down the Smith regime, which is unlikely, the only effect of present British policy would be to substitute another settler regime in place of the existing one. Ian Smith's unilateral declaration of independence was only one incident in a calculated policy of progressive oppression and degradation of the African people of the colony. The settler clique is quite capable of trading its present assumed independence for a settlement which would enable it to intensify its policy of repression. Unless the settler class are removed from power they will merely re-establish their authority under some nominally 'loyal' government and the situation which the African states have so often unanimously condemned when Southern Rhodesia was still a 'loyal' colony will be allowed to continue indefinitely.

The published correspondence and telephone conversations between the British prime minister and the rebel Smith show that the United Kingdom government were prepared to grant independence to Southern Rhodesia on the basis of the 1961 constitution provided that the settler regime would accept modifications allowing for only a gradual approach to majority rule. In other words, the United Kingdom government does not at heart accept the principle of the immediate majority rule for Southern Rhodesia to which it had agreed at the last Prime Ministers' Conference, and which all independent African states demand in accordance with the resolutions of the General Assembly of the United Nations. Even now the United Kingdom government has not revoked this 1961 constitution despite the fact that its power to do so remains unquestioned. Under this constitution the four million Africans of the colony are

THE INADEQUACY OF ECONOMIC SANCTIONS

condemned, in perpetuity, to be hewers of wood and carriers of water for 200,000 privileged European settlers. It is through this constitution that there are enforced and maintained laws which deprive the African inhabitants of any access to good farming land and which confine them to overcrowded and infertile reservations. Under these laws African domestic servants and farm labourers are compelled to serve their masters in conditions akin to slavery, and workers in industry have to live in appalling conditions in segregated townships and must accept a wage of less than one-tenth of that paid to Europeans who do a similar job. The African states have, through the Organisation of African Unity and individually, protested continuously against this intolerable state of affairs. The United Nations have passed resolution after resolution condemning conditions in Southern Rhodesia. Yet despite the fact that the United Kingdom parliament is now legislating for Southern Rhodesia, Britain has taken no step to set right any of these crying wrongs.

The government of Ghana believes that the United Kingdom government, if it wishes to convince African states of its sincerity, should revoke immediately the 1961 constitution of Southern Rhodesia and repeal the main discriminatory legislation, that is to say the Land Apportionment Act, the Vagrancy Act, the Pass Laws and other oppressive measures. The United Kingdom government should also immediately revoke the restriction orders imposed on opponents of the rebel regime, African, Asian and European alike. Britain should recall all British subjects now serving in the armed forces and the police of the illegal regime. The present position in this regard is farcical. Smith and those supporting him have been condemned by Britain as traitors yet high ranking officers of the army, air force and police who are the mainstay of his illegal regime, are receiving pensions from Britain.

The Ghana government has always maintained that the best and most effective method of ending the Southern Rhodesian rebellion is by the use of armed force. The Ghana government believes that this armed force shall be provided by African states and that its use should be authorised by the United Nations. Even if economic sanctions were successful they would only provoke a situation in which armed force would have to be used. If rebel authority collapses there must be some military force available to maintain order and it would be intolerable if this were left to the same military and police personnel who had supported Smith's rebel regime. The government of Ghana, therefore, believes it is its duty to play its full part in any military intervention against Southern Rhodesia which may be decided upon.

The government of Ghana has taken note of the statement made in the British parliament by the United Kingdom prime minister on 21st December, 1965 in which he called attention to the fact that the rebels possessed their own armed forces and that therefore any attempt to subdue the rebellion by force would lead to a bloody war turning into a bloody civil war. The Ghana government has noted that any consideration of bloodshed has not previously deterred the United Kingdom government from taking action in Kenya, Cyprus or British Guiana. The government of Ghana, however, does not believe that any such result would follow from the use of force in Southern Rhodesia. If the use of force produced that result, the entire responsibility for the situation would rest with the government of the United Kingdom. In 1963 the United Kingdom government vetoed in the Security Council of the United Nations a resolution sponsored by Ghana and supported by all the independent African states which would have prevented the arming of the Southern Rhodesian settlers. The armed forces, which the British prime minister now considers capable of preventing the United Kingdom government taking any effective action against rebels, were only two years ago handed over to the Smith regime by the British government on its own responsibility, and despite the fact that the Security Council had overwhelmingly voted against this being done. This fact alone, in the view of the government of Ghana, imposes an obligation on the United Kingdom government to disarm and disband at once the rebel troops upon which the illegal settler regime of Ian Smith depends.

In any case the Ghana government believes that the United Kingdom government has no longer any justification in con-

THE INADEQUACY OF ECONOMIC SANCTIONS

tinuing to claim that events in Southern Rhodesia are solely an internal British question. The United Kingdom has allowed a rebel regime to take power. The British government has ceased to have any control over the situation. In the government of Ghana's opinion the proper organisation to deal now with Southern Rhodesia is the Organisation of African Unity acting under the authority of the United Nations and with the support, if necessary, of other friendly nations who have an interest in seeing the revolt suppressed and in seeing established a Rhodesian constitution based upon the principles laid down by the General Assembly of the United Nations which include the principle of 'one man one vote'.

If economic sanctions are to be applied this can only be done effectively under the charter of the United Nations. The Ghana government has noted that the United Kingdom government has opposed the Southern Rhodesian situation being dealt with under the charter. It has continually claimed that Southern Rhodesia is an internal British question and at the last meeting of the Security Council the United Kingdom opposed action under chapter VII of the charter which is the only chapter under which sanctions can be made mandatory on all countries.

The present position is that the United Kingdom government claims the right to decide what economic sanctions shall be imposed and what economic sanctions shall not be imposed. The British government has appealed to all countries to adopt these sanctions at the same time well knowing that any such appeal will be ignored by South Africa and Portugal. Again, if the United Kingdom government wishes to convince African states of its sincerity it should at once convene a meeting of the Security Council and propose at that meeting that mandatory sanctions are imposed against Southern Rhodesia under chapter VII, Article 41 of the charter. The government of Ghana regards it as hypocrisy for the United Kingdom government to ask African states to impose sanctions against Southern Rhodesia while at the same time the British government refuses to use the machinery of the United Nations to make these sanctions effective or to do anything to prevent them being flouted by Portugal, Britain's oldest ally, and South Africa, one of her principal trading partners. In the event of the British government failing to do its duty in this regard the government of Ghana will confer with other African states as to how best the matter can be raised in the Security Council independently of Britain.

In considering generally the Southern Rhodesian situation, in the Ghana government's view, one fundamental fact should always be borne in mind. Everywhere on the African continent where a European minority has been in power, the African majority has been ill-treated and oppressed. Nowhere on the African continent where an African majority has been in authority have the European minority been molested or discriminated against.

The solution to the Southern Rhodesian question, therefore, in the Ghana government's opinion, lies in establishing majority rule in Southern Rhodesia at the earliest possible moment. The government of Ghana does not accept the contention of the United Kingdom government that while the people of Bechuanaland are capable of independence those of Southern Rhodesia are not. In its view if the Africans living on the northern bank of the Zambezi River have shown themselves fully capable of running an independent state then there is no reason to suppose that those living immediately south of that river are not equally capable of so doing. If they are not then it is the final indictment of the settler regime of Southern Rhodesia which for the last forty-three years has had exclusive control over African education in the colony. Settler rule, in the view of the government of Ghana, stands condemned and cannot be allowed to continue in any form whatsoever. Once again, if the United Kingdom wish to convince African states of its sincerity, it must declare forthwith that once the settler revolt has been crushed, settler rule will be ended for all time.

The Ghana government believes that the United Kingdom government has lost all control over the Southern Rhodesian situation and further is unwilling to take any of the steps by which its authority might be reasserted. In such circumstances, it is time for those more determined and more capable than

Britain to take charge. It is time that the United Nations declared that the Southern Rhodesian situation was a danger to world peace and invited the African states to carry out the task which the United Kingdom is unable or unwilling to perform.

11

RHODESIA, AN AFRICAN VIEW

In January 1966, a conference of Commonwealth heads of government was held in Lagos to consider the Rhodesian situation. Nkrumah did not attend. In declining the invitation he declared that no useful purpose could be served by such a conference. The settler regime could only be ended by firm action including the use of force, and this had been ruled out in advance by the British government.

As events proved, the Lagos conference achieved nothing. Shortly after it ended the Nigerian government was overthrown in a military coup, and the head of state, Balewa, was murdered.

It was just before the January 1966 coup took place in Nigeria that Nkrumah wrote the article entitled Rhodesia, an African view, which was subsequently published in the English magazine Punch on 23 February 1966. On the day after it was published, 24 February 1966, the CPP government in Ghana was itself toppled in a military coup.

The article, written specifically for a British magazine, first informs the readership of the basic facts of the situation within Rhodesia, and then goes on to consider how majority rule can be achieved in the shortest possible time. Nkrumah knew that the African people of Rhodesia would win their freedom through their own endeavours in time. But he thought that the process could be speeded up through 'military action from outside', preferably through the OAU acting on the authority of the UN. Referring to the settler regime he wrote: 'It is only a matter of time when it shall fall. Its overthrow will only be the first stage in the total liberation of southern Africa.' When the article was written, the coup in Portugal of

RHODESIA, AN AFRICAN VIEW

1974 could not have been foreseen, and it seemed likely that the African majority in Rhodesia would achieve independence before the peoples of the Portuguese colonies of Angola and Mozambique.

Article by Nkrumah published in *Punch*, 23 February 1966

Much of the controversy in Britain about Southern Rhodesia appears to us in Africa to be irrelevant. The exercise of political power by the African majority of the people of Southern Rhodesia is inevitable. An African government is the only effective way of ending the exploitation and degradation of the African peoples of the territory.

The arguments now being put forward in Britain against the principle of 'one man one vote' in regard to Southern Rhodesia are identical, even in terms, to the resistance put up against the British franchise in the nineteenth century to the British working classes. The arguments used in the case of Southern Rhodesia can be answered in the words of Joseph Chamberlain, addressed in 1884 to British agricultural workers who at that time were denied the right to vote – *'If you were turbulent they would say you were unfit for liberty; and as you are orderly and peaceful, they dare to say you do not want it.'*

Arguments about whether or not Africans in Southern Rhodesia are fit to rule are as inconsequential as the nineteenth-century arguments used to debar the British agricultural worker from exercising his right to vote. It is only through the ordinary man having the right to vote that he can exercise constitutional pressures for changes in the social system. When a social system becomes as diseased as that of Southern Rhodesia, a point is reached where the only alternative to constitutional change is a violent revolution. Constitutional change is impossible so long as power is left in the hands of a privileged minority of the population. In fact the situation in Southern Rhodesia had already reached explosion point long before UDI. Constitutional government, even on the basis of all power being in the hands of the European minority, could no longer provide the machinery for repression which was necessary. UDI is thus merely one symptom of the deep seated malady of the regime. The only effective answer, therefore, to UDI is the forcible overthrow of the regime which conceived it.

The sheet-anchor of settler power in Southern Rhodesia is the notorious Land Apportionment Act. In a country, still largely agricultural, this Act reserves in perpetuity all the best farming land for some 220,000 Europeans and confines the four million African inhabitants to the infertile and unhealthy middle and low veldts. Out of the 85 million acres of farmland in Rhodesia, the European settlers are allotted almost one half in extent: 41 million acres go to them and only 44 million acres to the African inhabitants who outnumber them by the ratio of 16 to 1. The European farms are immense in size: over one-third of the European holdings consist of farms of more than 20,000 acres in extent. All land occupied by the European settlers is consistently under-farmed, only some three to four per cent of it being fully cultivated. In contrast, the African farms are small and declining in productivity because they must be of necessity overfarmed.

The consequences can be seen from the 1962 census, conducted by the settlers themselves. Half the African population are shown as living in the so called 'Tribal Trust Lands'. The percentage of adult males, however, living in these Tribal Trust Lands is only 17·4 per cent, as compared with a percentage of 45·2 per cent of adult males among the African urban population. In other words, the Land Apportionment Act not only impoverishes the African inhabitants; it also breaks up all family life, and forces adult male workers into the towns or on to European farms where they must labour under conditions which are insufferable.

The average monthly wage of an African agricultural labourer is £5 3s. A European worker who does comparable work receives on average £108 a month. An African miner is paid an average wage of £12 a month, a European miner receives £138. The treatment of African domestic servants, of whom there are some 80,000, is little short of slavery. There are no schools for their children. Husbands and wives are not allowed to live together or have their children with them. A servant cannot see a film, go to a dance, attend an athletic event, hear a lecture or go for a walk at night. If he stays at home, and drinks an alcoholic beverage, he is guilty of criminal offence, for which he can be punished by a term of imprisonment.

Similar conditions apply to most of the industrial workers. They are compelled to live in African *locations* where, as often as not, they are separated from their families. Eighty per cent of the accommodation provided for the African workers of Salisbury is for single men. Usually four men are compelled to live and cook in one small room. The African town worker may only have a visitor to stay with him if he obtains the permission of the Superintendent of a location; he may only leave his lodging for two weeks, unless he obtains special permission; and in general, may not be out of doors after 9 p.m. He automatically loses his home if he is dismissed by his employer, or if he is convicted of any political offence, or even if he transgresses some of the provisions of the *Pass* Laws. Six years ago the Roman Catholic hierarchy in Rhodesia thus summed up the position:

> '... *Wages are inadequate, housing conditions in many instances are unworthy of human beings, and terms of employment are such that husbands are separated for long periods from their wives.*
>
> *Such a state of affairs cries to heaven for vengeance and even in the natural order can only breed crime and chaos ...*'

This state of affairs was not created by the Smith regime. It is part and parcel of the settler system which no individual settler of group or settlers, however well intentioned, can overturn. For example, I have known personally for many years Mr Garfield Todd, who was one of our guests at the Ghana independence celebrations. He is a man of the greatest goodwill and was, at the time we attained independence, prime minister of Southern Rhodesia. Yet even in this position of power he was not able to do anything. During his term of office the United States author, John Gunther, visited Southern Rhodesia and wrote afterwards about conditions under Mr Todd's regime. He said:

RHODESIA FILE

> *'There are, no doubt, honest English people who have a sentimental attachment to Rhodesia, and for that matter honest Rhodesians who have no basis of comparison with other countries and who are blind to what is happening under their noses, ignorant of the fact that racial discriminations in Rhodesia are among the most barbarous, shameful, and disgusting in the world.'*

This same blindness as to the facts seems to affect Britain today. The idea which appears to be prevalent is that all that is required to be done is to replace one set of *'disloyal'* settlers by another set of *'loyal'* settlers. But if Mr Garfield Todd, during the five years he was prime minister, could not change in any significant respect the racial structure of the colony, how can anyone seriously imagine it can be changed by Rhodesia's present governor, Sir Humphrey Gibbs, or by any group of settlers he might appoint as an alternative government?

It is true that there were, before UDI, numerous and influential opponents of the Smith regime among the European settlers. These individuals included the most far-seeing and intelligent elements in the European minority. Their quarrel with the Rhodesian Front, however, was not about how to change the existing social structure. It was about how best to preserve it. Those who opposed UDI among the Europeans considered that they could practise apartheid and oppression much more safely under the shadow of the Union Jack, than as a nominally independent country, relying for external support upon South Africa and Portugal, which was the aim of the Smith regime.

Now that UDI is a reality it is, in my view, quite mistaken to suppose that these former opponents of the Rhodesian Front policy can be rallied to support an alternative European government. From their point of view the only basis for such a government would be the continuation intact of the pre-UDI social system, and they are intelligent enough to realise that this could not be done once there was a split amongst the settlers. Foolish as they may think Smith's action was, they have now no choice but to go along with him. It is for this reason that I believe the only effective alternative government will be one based upon majority rule: one man one vote.

RHODESIA, AN AFRICAN VIEW

The Southern Rhodesian problem will never be solved so long as the colony's institutions are based on legally enforced inequality and apartheid. Yet the whole object of the so called *'Rhodesian self-government'* principle, that is to say, rule by the settler minority without control or interference by Britain, was to perpetuate the existing system of oppression. For this reason a return to the 1961 constitution, which some people in Britain appear to believe is all that is necessary, would merely aggravate the existing explosive situation. The 1961 constitution must therefore be revoked forthwith.

As I have said on a number of occasions, I cannot understand the argument that while Africans on one side of the Zambesi are capable of self-government those on the other side are not, and that while Bechuanaland is ready for independence on the basis of universal suffrage, Southern Rhodesia is not. I believe that the apparent absurdity of this argument arises from a confusion between two quite different things, namely on the one hand, the right of the Africans of Southern Rhodesia to have a government of their own choice, and on the other hand the ability of Africans in Southern Rhodesia to provide the administrative machinery for such a government.

It is true, of course, that insufficient Africans have been trained for administrative posts. It is equally true that so long as the settlers control the government, Africans will continue to be denied the opportunity of this training. As long as the Rhodesian Front policy remains in vogue and in power, it is impossible to expect a liberal programme of education and training for Africans to be enforced with the object of producing the African cadres which can take over power from the settlers in their lifetime. In order therefore to Africanise the administrative machinery, it is necessary to have a government controlled by the African majority. Ian Smith makes a lot of play of the fact that the chiefs in Southern Rhodesia assist the government in the administration of the country. If this is true, why can't the chiefs join the neutral government? It is however well known that the chiefs would not be allowed by the white settlers to play so prominent a role. At any rate the Africans cannot agree that the chiefs should represent them in the government. The

Africans still support their political leaders who should be released from restriction. The UN and OAU have called for their release. It is the duty and responsibility of Britain to ensure that this is done.

As an interim measure after independence, other independent African states could supply the civil servants, technicians and specialists required and probably also the necessary senior military and police officers. In any event, the military and police forces which have supported the rebellion would have to be disarmed and completely reorganised.

However, who rules Southern Rhodesia immediately after the revolt is quelled will depend upon who suppresses the rebellion. I have always held the view that the Smith regime will not be destroyed by sanctions. Sanctions, however, if universally applied, might be a contributing factor in producing a successful takeover of power by the African inhabitants of the colony. If a civil war broke out in Southern Rhodesia between the European minority and the African majority, I doubt whether any independent African state would agree to provide facilities in its territory for British troops to restore 'law and order' in the colony. The United Kingdom government, having refused to use military force to suppress the European rebels, cannot now claim the right to send in defence forces in order to rescue these same rebels from their opponents. If the African population requires assistance in dealing with the settlers then the right body to provide that assistance is the Organisation of African Unity, acting under the authority of the United Nations.

In the event of sanctions not provoking a takeover of power by the African majority, what then? Clearly, the only remaining course is military action from outside. Again this should be by the Organisation of African Unity acting under the authority of the United Nations. From press reports of what was said by the British prime minister to those Commonwealth Heads of Government who attended the Lagos Conference, it appears that Mr Wilson was advised that the Southern Rhodesia rebels had very substantial forces under their command. On paper this is true. In 1963 Britain vetoed a resolution of the Security Council, not opposed by any other member, which would have prevented the arming of the Smith regime. In consequence, the Rhodesian Front government which was already in power, and already talking about UDI, was presented with the weapons and aircraft which enabled it to carry out its threatened revolt. The strength of these weapons should not be underestimated. On the other hand, one should not, as Mr Wilson appears to have done at Lagos, overrate them. Mr Wilson seemed to have assumed that the Southern Rhodesian rebels could deploy an army 27,000 strong, and that it would be necessary to make a frontal attack on this army across the Zambesi river. In the first place, this figure of 27,000 troops is obtained by adding to the regular military forces the police and the large European police reserve which in fact forms the greater part of the total. The question which must be asked is how much of this force would in fact be available to meet any military action from outside. The key to the Southern Rhodesian situation is the extent of internal unrest. The armed forces of the Ian Smith rebels and their police are already tied down by the threat of local risings against their illegal regime; it is unlikely therefore that the rebels could commit more than a fraction of their forces to guard their frontiers against invasion from abroad.

If the United Kingdom government had seriously considered military action, the territories from which it could have been mounted include Bechuanaland, which has a far longer frontier with Southern Rhodesia than Zambia, and so-called Portuguese Mozambique. If the United Kingdom Government had seriously wished to suppress the rebellion by force, it would have invoked the ancient Anglo-Portuguese Treaties which permitted Britain to use the Azores as a naval and military base during the last World War.

Military action against Southern Rhodesia by no means necessarily involves the occupation of the whole country; 63 per cent of the power on which the colony depends is derived from coal, mined in the Wankie Coalfields which lie close to the Zambian and Bechuanaland frontiers; 27 per cent of Rhodesia's power requirements only are provided by petroleum, and only 10 per cent is derived from the Kariba dam. Thus, even if oil sanctions were completely successful, the rebels would only be deprived of 27 per cent of their power requirements, but the military occupation of Wankie would cripple the colony economically.

Undoubtedly, the Ian Smith illegal regime will collapse and be overthrown. It is only a matter of time when it shall fall. Its overthrow will only be the first stage in the total liberation of southern Africa. The only question is how its fall can come about. It is high time that all men of goodwill considered soberly this Rhodesian issue. Action must be taken now to bring about a speedy and sensible transition to majority rule and thus save the risk of a violent conflict and a war with the possibility of escalation.

12

'A SHORT, SHARP AND FIRM CAMPAIGN'

The CPP government of Ghana was overthrown on 24 February 1966 and replaced by a reactionary military and police regime. Nkrumah was at the time on his way to Hanoi at the invitation of President Ho Chi Minh with proposals for ending the war in Vietnam. News of the coup was brought to him in Peking where he was scheduled to spend a few days en route to Hanoi. Nkrumah has given an account of the Ghana coup and his views of the internal and external forces behind it in his book Dark Days in Ghana.* *This book also contains a full account of what subsequently happened in Ghana as the so-called National Liberation Council (NLC) proceeded to reverse the socialist and Pan-African policies of the CPP government.*

Nkrumah's first reaction on hearing of the coup was to return at once to Ghana. But knowing that he could not get back within twenty-four hours, the time within which he thought he might be able to avoid unnecessary bloodshed, he decided instead to accept the invitation of President Sékou Touré of Guinea and go to Conakry. He arrived there on 2 March 1966 to an ecstatic welcome from the people of Guinea. At a mass rally on the following day, Sékou Touré presented Nkrumah to the people of Guinea as Secretary-General of the Parti Démocratique de Guinée (PDG) and head of state of Guinea. It was a magnificent and unprecedented act of Pan-Africanism, and reflected the admiration for Nkrumah and solidarity of the people of Guinea with all he represented. During the period of CPP government, Nkrumah had several times

* First published in 1968 by Panaf Books Ltd.

RHODESIA FILE

visited Guinea, and in 1958 when Guinea refused to join de Gaulle's French Community and was in severe financial difficulties, Nkrumah provided funds to tide them over. There had followed the Ghana–Guinea Union and the development of a very special sense of brotherhood between Nkrumah and Sékou Touré, who held the same views on African liberation and unification.

In Conakry, Nkrumah at once set up an office and proceeded to continue his work to advance the African revolution, and at the same time to prepare for his return to Ghana. One of his first actions was to arrange for the installation of a wireless station at Villa Syli, his residence in Conakry. Through this he was kept fully informed of world news and of events inside Ghana.

On hearing of the victory of the British Labour Party in the general election of 1966, he characteristically took the opportunity of writing to prime minister Harold Wilson on the Rhodesian situation. The text of his letter follows. The only response from Wilson was a few lines of formal acknowledgement signed by his secretary.

Letter to Harold Wilson on the Rhodesian situation, written by Nkrumah in Conakry on 11 April 1966

Dear Prime minister,

Pressure of work has prevented me writing to you earlier to congratulate you on your victory in the General Election.

I was particularly pleased to see that the seat in Smethwick which had previously been lost because of a virulent racialistic campaign was returned to Labour with a resounding majority and also, for the same reason, that Mr Patrick Gordon-Walker was returned this time for Leyton. These two victories will have restored faith that the British people as a whole do not wish their society to be infected with racialism.

Most of us in Africa instinctively feel a sympathy with the Labour Party as the mass party of the working class and we are well aware that a Conservative victory would have been very damaging to our cause in Africa.

I noticed that the Conservative Party introduced the question of Rhodesia into their election campaign and made it obvious

'A SHORT, SHARP AND FIRM CAMPAIGN'

that had they secured a victory they would have lost no time in seeking negotiations with the Smith regime that would without doubt have resulted in an early betrayal of the position of the African majority in that country. I was also glad to know that the Labour spokesmen reiterated their pledge that there would be no surrender of independence to a minority government, but that the future of the African majority would be safeguarded.

I am therefore very glad that the majority which you have now obtained will secure your Party firmly in power for a full term of office and perhaps, if I may say so, enable you to act with a greater firmness and independence than may have been the case during the last seventeen months.

You know my views on the question of Rhodesia and I do not need to argue them again. It is my view that this question cannot be resolved without firm action including the use of force to restore constitutional government in Rhodesia and open the way to a constitutional conference and the establishment of independence on the basis of majority rule. Every independent African government has basically this same view and I think it fair to say that all of us in Africa believe that any further prevarication with the Smith rebel regime can only endanger peace and lead to a catastrophic division of the world along racial lines.

It is obvious that Ian Smith is being aided and abetted by South Africa and Portugal in his effort to survive the economic sanctions which have been imposed and that such a method of trying to resolve the problem is likely to be long-drawn-out and to lead to unnecessary suffering for the general population and increasing bitterness on the side of the Africans in Rhodesia and the independent African states. Every African has a sense of identity with his brother Africans in Rhodesia and finds it difficult to understand why the British government which has settled much less difficult problems with speed and efficiency hesitates to employ military methods in the case of Rhodesia unless it is simply because the rebel government happens to be composed of Europeans.

My view is that a straight warning should be given to the Smith government that if they do not abandon their rebellion forthwith and agree to participate in a constitutional conference to which all sections of the community are invited, then force will be used without further notice. A short, sharp and firm campaign would end this dangerous situation with far less suffering and bitterness than is likely as a result of a policy of economic sanctions and I hope that you and your government will give this matter some new consideration now that your more pressing domestic difficulties have been resolved by your overwhelming electoral victory and the massive vote of confidence which the British people have given to you.

13

ZIMBABWE

Nkrumah lived in Conakry from March 1966 until August 1971 when he was compelled to go to Bucarest for medical treatment. It was reported that he had cancer, and he died in Bucarest on 27 April 1972.

During the Conakry period Nkrumah wrote five books and five pamphlets. The books were Dark Days in Ghana; Axioms *(Freedom Fighters' Edition);* Handbook of Revolutionary Warfare; Class Struggle in Africa; Revolutionary Path; *and the pamphlets were* The Spectre of Black Power; The Struggle Continues; Ghana: The Way Out; The Big Lie; Two Myths.

In addition, he revised Consciencism, *and broadcast regularly to the people of Ghana between March and December 1966. The texts of the broadcasts were subsequently printed in paperback by Panaf Books under the title* Voice from Conakry.

The extracts which follow, taken from the books and pamphlets written while he was in Conakry, show the development of his thought on the whole question of minority regimes which he always saw in the wider context of the complete liberation and unification of Africa. He analysed the growing class conflict in Africa, and emphasised the need to use all forms of struggle, including armed force, to free the whole African population from every type of oppression. Nkrumah foresaw the eventual political unification of Africa and a 'unified socialist society in which the African Personality will find full expression'.

* From the Conclusion to *Revolutionary Path* the last book to be written by Nkrumah. Published by Panaf Books posthumously in 1973.

Nkrumah's ideas have survived him and gained wider acceptance. The mass of the people of Africa are committed to the complete liberation of the continent; and many more than when he was alive now share Nkrumah's view that political unification on a socialist basis is the essential framework for the development of Africa in the interests of all Africans.

Extracts concerning settler politics and the liberation of southern Africa from books and pamphlets written by Nkrumah during the Conakry period 1966–71
Axioms of Kwame Nkrumah (Freedom Fighters' Edition), (1967) pp. 61, 64, 65, 68, 76, 79, 101-2, 114, 117, 119, 120.

The right of people to decide their own destiny, to make their way in freedom, is not to be measured by the yardstick of colour or degree of social development. It is an inalienable right of peoples which they are powerless to exercise when forces stronger than they themselves, by whatever means, for whatever reasons, take this right away from them. (*Motion of Destiny Speech*, 10 July 1953)

When I talk of freedom and independence for Africa, I mean that the vast African majority should be accepted as forming the basis of government in Africa. (*I speak of Freedom*, p. 175)

Statesmen have broadcast the need to respect fundamental freedoms, the right of men to live free from the shadow of fears which cramp their dignity when they exist in servitude, in poverty, in degradation and contempt. They proclaimed the Atlantic Charter and the Charter of the United Nations, and then said that all these had no reference to the enslaved world outside the limits of imperialism and racial arrogance. (*Africa Must Unite*, Introduction, p. xi)

When all is said and done, it is the so-called little man, the bent-backed, exploited, malnourished, blood-covered fighter for independence who decides. And he invariably decides for freedom. (*Neocolonialism*, p. 254)

The right of a people to govern themselves is a fundamental principle, and to compromise on this principle is to betray it. (*Motion of Destiny Speech*, 10 July 1953)

If there is to be a criterion of a people's preparedness for self-government, then I say it is their readiness to assume the responsibility of ruling themselves. For who but a people themselves can say when they are prepared? (*The same*)

What right has any colonial power to expect Africans to become 'Europeans' or to have 100 per cent literacy before it considers them 'ripe' for self-government? Wasn't the African, who is now considered 'unprepared' to govern himself, 'governing' himself before the advent of Europeans? (*Towards Colonial Freedom*, p. 37)

To the African, the European settler, whether living in South Africa, Kenya, Angola, or anywhere else in Africa, is an intruder, an alien who has seized African land. No amount of arguing about the so-called benefits of European rule can alter the fundamental right of Africans to order their own affairs. (*Africa Must Unite*, p. 10)

All that we are asking for is that in Africa the majority should form the basis of government. (*Press conference in New Delhi*, 29 December 1958)

The authority to govern a state should spring from the people, and the people's right to exercise these powers is based on the principle of one man one vote. (*Broadcast on 3rd anniversary of Independence, March 1960*)

So long as any group on this continent denies the principle of one man one vote, and uses its power to maintain its privilege, there will be insecurity for the oppressors and constant resentment and revolt on the part of the oppressed. (*Speech of welcome at Conference to discuss Positive Action and Security in Africa, Accra, 7 April 1960*)

No government can continue to impose its rule in the face of the conscious defiance of the overwhelming masses of its people. There is no force, however impregnable, that a united and determined people cannot overcome. (*The same*)

What the ruling minorities should be afraid of is not that power will fall into the hands of the majority, but that by their own attempt to maintain a social order which can no longer exist, they will themselves be their own executioners. (*Speech in Dublin, 18 May 1960*)

The first step towards testing the right of rule in communities of mixed races and creeds is to give every adult, irrespective of race and creed the right to vote. When each citizen thereby enjoys equality of status with all the others, barriers of race and colour will disappear and the people will mix freely together and will work for the common good. (*Africa Must Unite*, p. 11)

There is no logic except the right of might that can accept the undemocratic rule of a majority by a minority. The predominant racial group must, and will, provide the government of a country. (*The same*)

ZIMBABWE

Settlers, provided they accept the principle of one man one vote, and majority rule, may be tolerated; but settler minority governments, never. They are a dangerous anachronism, and must be swept away completely and for ever. (*Handbook of Revolutionary Warfare*, p. 46)

The foulest intellectual rubbish ever invented by man is that of racial superiority and inferiority. (*Speech made in Accra*, 21 June 1952)

I do not believe in racialism and tribalism. The concept 'Africa for the Africans' does not mean that other races are excluded from it. *(Speech made in Monrovia during state visit, January 1953)*

We repudiate and condemn all forms of racialism, for racialism not only injures those against whom it is used, but warps and perverts the very people who preach and project it. *(Speech of welcome at Accra Conference of Independent African States, 15 April 1958)*

Taking up arms for African freedom and unity is not the product of a cruel, uncouth purpose, it is an art, the crystallisation of serious study and knowledge of the oppressor and the oppressed. *(Handbook of Revolutionary Warfare, prelims)*

Revolutionary warfare is the logical, inevitable answer to the political, economic and social situation in Africa today. Either we fight now, or we will each fall in turn unaided and alone to the collective blows of imperialism. (*The same*, p. 42)

Time is on the side of the masses, and nothing can permanently frustrate their ultimate fulfilment. (*The Struggle Continues*, p. 45)

Challenge of the Congo. Author's note written in Conakry, 1 June 1969

Since *Challenge of the Congo* was first published in 1967, conflict between progressive and reactionary forces in Africa has sharpened. A point has now been reached where armed struggle is the only way through which African revolutionaries can achieve their objectives. Recent events in Africa have exposed the fallacy of trying to banish imperialism, neocolonialism and settler regimes from our continent by peaceful means. The aggression of the enemies of Africa continues, and has become more ruthless and insidious. The evidence is all around us.

There has been a succession of military *coups d'etat* in which some of our few remaining progressive leaders have been removed from the political scene. In Nigeria, a civil war fanned by imperialists and neocolonialists for their own interests, is sapping vital energy which should be directed to the building up of Africa's political and economic strength. In Rhodesia, the fascist settler government is still imposing its reactionary policies on the African majority; and the claim that the imposition of economic sanctions would topple the regime has been proved false. As for the Congo, the murderers of Patrice Lumumba still go unpunished; and Pierre Mulele, one of Africa's most experienced freedom fighters, who was tricked into returning to Kinshasa, has been executed by the agents of neocolonialism. Further examples of imperialist and neocolonialist aggression are too numerous to mention.

And so the challenge of the Congo remains, and crises continue to occur as the African revolutionary struggle gains momentum. It is a call to arms; and a call for the co-ordination and the centralisation of all our efforts in a fight to the death against an aggressive and determined enemy.

We must combine strategy and tactics, and establish political and military machinery for the prosecution of the African revolutionary war. It is only in this way that the aspirations of the African masses can be achieved, and an All-African Union Government be established in a totally free and united Africa.

ZIMBABWE

Handbook of Revolutionary Warfare (1968), Book One, KNOW THE ENEMY, pp. 18-21, and p. 23.

Imperialists are not content with trying to convince us that we are politically immature. They are telling us, now that we are realising that armed revolution is the only way to defeat neo-colonialism, that we are inherently incapable of fighting a successful revolutionary war.

This new psychological propaganda campaign is being waged in various subtle ways. First, there is what may be called the 'moral' argument; Africans are constantly being reminded that they are a peace-loving, tolerant and communalist-minded people. The African is projected as an individual who has always been loath to shed blood. The corollary to this argument is that it would be immoral and against our nature to engage in revolutionary warfare.

The moral argument is easily destroyed. Centuries of liberation wars, wars of conquest, revolution and counter-revolution in the west were not considered to be moral or immoral. They were simply part of western historical development. *Our armed struggle for freedom is neither moral nor immoral, it is a scientific historically determined necessity.*

The second argument used to deflect us from the inevitability of armed struggle is the so-called 'economy' argument. It runs something like this; modern neocolonialism does not constitute a danger to young, revolutionary African states, and therefore the military training and arming of the broad masses is an expensive and frivolous enterprise. The corollary of this reactionary argument is; since you cannot, in the present under-developed state of your economy afford the 'luxury' of your own defence, let us take care of it for you. And the trap is set.

Last but not least, is a third series of racialist and defeatist arguments designed to spread the myth that no African revolutionary is capable of carrying an armed struggle through to the end. It condemns *a priori* all African revolutionary activities to failure. It wraps revolutionary warfare on our continent in an aura of disparagement, and tries to cripple us with a sense of inadequacy as freedom fighters.

By means of press and radio, accounts are given of the capture of 'terrorists' by 'security forces' (note the choice of words), the 'terrorists' being usually described as poorly trained, ill-equipped, demoralised and uncertain of the cause for which they are fighting. When arms and military equipment are seized, it is always labelled 'Russian' or 'Chinese', to suggest that the freedom fighters who use them are not African nationalists, but the dupes and tools of foreign governments.

When freedom fighters are captured and tried in courts of law, they are treated as criminals, not as prisoners of war, and are imprisoned, shot or hanged, usually after so-called confessions have been extorted. This refusal to recognise freedom fighters as soldiers is again part of imperialist strategy designed to pour scorn on the armed revolutionary movement, and at the same time to discourage further recruits.

The campaign is based on the counter-insurgency law whereby 'it is necessary to attack the revolution during the initial stages of the movement when it is still weak, when it has not yet fulfilled that which should be its main aspiration – a total integration with the people' (Che Guevara). This is why we are being told that Africans are incapable of sustaining revolutionary warfare:

a. racially
b. because of our historical background
c. for lack of cadres, ideology and leadership.

In one breath, we are accused of being too primitive to govern ourselves, and in the next we are accused of not being primitive enough to wage guerrilla warfare!

The problem is not whether one is born or is not born a natural revolutionary fighter. The problem is not whether revolutionaries are naturally suited to Africa, or Africa to revolutionary warfare. Predestination of this sort never exists. The fact is that revolutionary warfare is the key to African freedom and is the only way in which the total liberation and unity of the African continent can be achieved.

ZIMBABWE

THE NEED FOR PAN-AFRICAN ORGANISATION

The independent states of Africa are militarily weak. Unlike the imperialists and neocolonialists they have no mutual defence system and no unified command to plan and direct joint action. But this will be remedied with the formation of the All-African People's Revolutionary Army and the setting up of organisations to extend and plan revolutionary warfare on a continental scale.

We possess the vital ingredient necessary to win – the full and enthusiastic support of the broad masses of the African people who are determined once and for all to end all forms of foreign exploitation, to manage their own affairs, and to determine their own future. Against such overwhelming strength organised on a Pan-African basis, no amount of enemy forces can hope to succeed.

. . . . . .

OUR OBJECTIVES (pp. 34–35)

Since 1960, the struggle of the African people and the more or less latent state of crisis inside many African territories have reached maturity. To counter-balance the growing revolutionary character of the African situation, the enemy's reaction has become more open and direct. Both the Algerian and the Congolese wars were born of the people's determination to free themselves at whatever cost, the only difference being that the Algerian revolt developed in an essentially colonial context, whereas the Congolese struggle is being waged in a neocolonialist setting, marked by major imperialist aggression throughout the African continent.

From a practical point of view, the differences between the various segments of the liberation struggle in time and space are minimal. The only factors which render the Congolese, Angolan and Rhodesian struggles (to take these examples only) more violent than others are, first, the escalation of imperialist action;

and secondly, the more advanced nature of the people's organisation, though the actual level of readiness to revolt may be just as high elsewhere.

. . . . . .

THE ORGANISATION OF AFRICAN UNITY (OAU) (pp. 36–37)

The militant African forces did achieve a certain amount of success when all blocs and groups joined together to form the OAU at Addis Ababa in 1963. However, appearances are sometimes deceptive: the dissolution of pro-imperialist groups did not mean that the interests they represented also vanished.

On the contrary, an examination of recent events exposes serious weaknesses within the OAU. The Organisation failed to solve the crisis in the Congo and Rhodesia: both of them test cases – the former involving a direct challenge to neocolonialism, and the latter open confrontation with a minority, settler government. In fact, the OAU is in danger of developing into a useful cover for the continued, sterile action of conflicting interests, the only difference being, that in the context of one big 'brotherly' organisation reactionary tactics are camouflaged and applied through the subtleties of negotiation.

This change of tactics works as strongly as ever against the fundamental interests of progressive forces in Africa, since it hides concessions to imperialism.

Negotiations are concluded behind closed doors and surrounded by a mysterious cloak of diplomatic protocol, making knowledge of the proceedings inaccessible to the general public.

However, four explosive issues discussed at the OAU Conference in Accra in 1965, alerted progressive opinion to the dangers of continued compromise:

a. the crisis in Rhodesia
b. the struggle in the Congo
c. the treatment of African political refugees
d. the problem of South West Africa

In the first place, the African heads of state failed to agree on a practical way of checking Ian Smith's rebellion, and instead fell back on the futile policy of negotiations with Britain combined with diplomatic pressure at international and UN level.

Similarly, in the Congo, the fundamental issue of the crisis was avoided in spite òf the tense situation resulting from the gallant stand of the freedom fighters carrying on the struggle in the spirit of Lumumba ...

The radical African states in the OAU were confronted with the difficulty of finding effective expression for the aspirations of the broad masses of the people.

Africa Day special message, 1968

As the armed phase of the African revolution for total liberation and unity gains momentum in central and southern Africa, racist settlers, imperialists and neocolonialists are intensifying and diversifying their efforts to consolidate and extend their domination. They are faced with a protracted guerrilla struggle which in the long run they know they cannot win. But they are seeking by joint military action to contain it, and by devious and insinuating economic and political penetration to undermine its strength. They see their opportunity in the continuing disunity of independent Africa, the lack of continental planning and direction of the liberation struggle, and in the willingness of certain African leaders to allow their countries to become client states. Collective imperialism confronts a disunited, weakened, independent Africa.

The situation demands immediate and drastic remedy. We must throw the full weight of a united, revolutionary Africa into the struggle. Each day that we delay, we fail our gallant freedom fighters and betray our people.

It is an open secret that South Africa, Portugal and Rhodesia are co-operating in the military sphere to crush guerrilla campaigns in their territories. They exchange information about freedom fighter activities, allow overflights and landings of military aircraft in each other's countries, and in the case of South Africa, supply armed forces and helicopters to assist in the counter-offensive. A military intelligence board, known as the

Council of Three, is said to meet regularly in Pretoria, Salisbury, Lourenco Marques or Luanda, to prepare joint action.

The world first heard of the participation of South African forces in military action outside their own borders in August 1967, when a strong force of freedom fighters went into action around the Wankie game reserve in Rhodesia. A large contingent of South African police in armoured cars was rushed to the scene. Since then, there have been innumerable reports of South African intervention. In Rhodesia, South West Africa, Angola and Mozambique, South African helicopters are being used to hunt freedom fighters. Armed South African police are operating against nationalists in South West Africa. South African troops are reported in both Angola and Mozambique. Nor is enemy co-operation confined to defensive operations. There are clear indications that the members of the Council of Three are planning offensive action against independent states. Zambia has been openly threatened. Furthermore, some ten miles from her border, on the Caprivi strip, the South Africans have built an enormous airfield, said to have a two-mile runway. There are many reports of armed incursions of Rhodesians, South Africans and Portuguese over the borders between Zambia, Rhodesia and Mozambique.

The example of the recent Israeli aggression against Arab states has not passed unnoticed in Pretoria, and has been publicly proclaimed in South Africa as an effective way of dealing with a so-called 'threat' from neighbouring states. Faced with the combined military strength of the South Africans, Portuguese and Rhodesian settlers, African freedom fighters must close their ranks and put an end to internecine rivalries. They must also be supported by united and determined action on the part of the whole of independent Africa.

No part of Africa is free while any of our national territory remains unliberated. There can be no co-existence between African independence and imperialist and neocolonialist domination; between independent Africa and racist, minority, settler governments.

The military obstacles we have to overcome if we are to achieve our goal of total liberation and an All-African Union

Government are obvious and surmountable. Less easy to recognise and to combat are the insidious, often disguised workings of neocolonialism – the economic and political pressures which seek to undermine our independence and to perpetuate and extend the grip of foreign monopoly finance capital over the economic life of our continent.

Many of our so-called independent states are in fact neo-colonies. They have all the outward appearance of sovereignty, but their economy and therefore their political policy is directed from outside. Some have been in the grip of neocolonialism since independence. Others have been subjected to neocolonialism by means of military coups engineered by neocolonialists acting in conjunction with indigenous reactionaries.

In recent months with the intensification of the guerrilla struggle in central and southern Africa, pressure has been strongly directed towards those states which have common frontiers with South Africa, Rhodesia, Angola and Mozambique. The object is to dominate them politically and economically, and thus hold up the advance of the African revolution and at the same time to improve their own neocolonialist position. The tragedy is that some African heads of state are themselves actually aiding and abetting imperialists and neocolonialists. In February 1967 Malawi became the first independent African state to conclude a trade agreement, and later to establish diplomatic relations with South Africa. Since then, other African states have also been lured into the South African neocolonialist web by a mixture of 'aid' and carefully veiled threats. The withdrawal of Britain from the High Commission territories, the break between Britain and Rhodesia as a result of UDI, and the outbreak of guerrilla warfare in the Portuguese colonies, has given South Africa a golden opportunity to jump in.

South Africa is in the classic, imperialist position of a manufacturing country seeking new outlets for its capital and goods. Its policy is to exploit the labour and resources of its hinterland, thereby strengthening South Africa's economy and at the same time delaying the advance of the African revolution.

South Africa's 'new policy' of improved relations with African states has been described as the building of 'bridges' rather than 'forts'. The crux of the matter was revealed clearly in the editorial of the South African 'Financial Gazette' of May 10, 1968:

'We must build more bridges and less forts. The might of our armed forces are not enough to shield off hostilities still being built up against South Africa in some African states. We must build more bridges into Africa. In Malawi we have virtually spanned a bridge into the heart of Africa.' A delighted broadcaster in Salisbury on October 8, 1967 praised Dr Banda for what he called his 'realistic policy', and added: 'the nations which are nearest to South Africa have been the quickest to realise the side on which their bread is buttered'. He referred here to Lesotho and Botswana.

South Africa is daily increasing her economic and political penetration into African territories. The Lesotho government in 1967 appointed three South Africans to 'advise' on political and economic affairs. In Rhodesia, South African capital investment already exceeds that of Britain; and it is mainly the support of South Africa which has enabled Ian Smith's rebel regime to survive.

The South African government has recently granted eight million rand to Malawi for the building of the new capital city at Lilongwe. Of the five million rand set aside for 'economic co-operation' two million has already been ear-marked for Malawi as a 'first instalment' this year. Since 1964, when Malawi became independent, imports from South Africa have doubled; while the main force behind capital investment in Malawi is increasingly the South African government itself.

The South African liberation movement together with the peoples of independent Africa and freedom fighters wherever they are operating must be alert to this new challenge. Neo-colonialism, like colonialism and imperialism can only be banished from our midst by armed struggle.

In east, central and west Africa, neocolonialism is hard at work fostering regional economic groupings, in the knowledge that without political cohesion they will remain weak and subject to neocolonialist pressures and domination. The US government in its latest statement on 'aid' has said that it will favour those states which are grouped together in this way.

As each new attempt is made to divide us and to divert us from our purpose, it must be exposed and attacked. Already, the ordinary men and women of Africa are talking the language of the African revolution. They speak of freedom, unity and socialism, and know that these objectives are synonymous, and can only be attained through armed struggle. In some cases, the people of Africa are ahead of their governments. But the pressures they are exerting will inevitably compel the pace forward.

We must recognise and fight the external and the internal enemy, and combine all our resources in the great struggle which lies ahead. With cohesive planning and with a full awareness of our united strength, nothing can halt the progress towards final victory.

Class Struggle in Africa (1970), CLASS CONCEPT, p. 21

The uneven economic development of Africa has made for a variety of class patterns with wide differences existing between the areas of white settler minority governments, the few remaining colonial enclaves, and independent Africa.

For example, in Rhodesia, four million Africans are crowded into less than half the land acreage of the country. In other words, more than half the land is in the hands of some 500,000 white settlers. This state of affairs has resulted in an enormous social and political gulf between the rich, white estate owners and the impoverished politically impotent African peasants and workers. Here, as in all settler areas, class is a race issue first and foremost – the 'haves' are white, the 'have-nots' are black – and all the usual arguments – the myth of racial inferiority, the need for government by the most able, and so on – are used to justify perpetuation of the enforced, racialist, settler arrangement.

PROLETARIAT, pp. 70–71

At present, Africa is one of the least developed continents in the world. It produces one-seventh of the world's raw materials, but only one fiftieth of the world's manufactures. The share of industry in Africa's total income is less than 14 per cent. This situation is a legacy of imperialism and colonialism, and the exploitation of Africa to serve the interests of international monopoly finance capital. But it is also a result of the continuing imperialist and capitalist exploitation of Africa through neocolonialism

Western monopolies still dominate about 80 per cent of the volume of African trade. A significant factor in recent times has been the rapid development of US penetration. Between 1951–55, direct US investments in Africa increased more than 2·5 times – from $313 to $793 million. Particularly deep penetration was made into South Africa, Rhodesia and Congo Kinshasa.

The methods of neocolonialism are economic control, in the form of 'aid', loans, trade and banking; the stranglehold of indigenous economies through vast international interlocking corporations; political direction through puppet governments; social penetration through the cultivation of an indigenous bourgeoisie, the imposition of 'defense' agreements, and the setting up of military and air bases; ideological expansion through the mass communications media of press, radio and television – the emphasis being on anti-communism; the fomenting of discord between countries and tribes; and through collective imperialism – notably the politico-economic and military co-operation of Rhodesia, South Africa and Portugal.

. . . . . .

PEASANTRY, pp. 75–76

In Africa, the peasantry is by far the largest contingent of the working class, and potentially the main force for socialist revolution. But it is dispersed, unorganised, and for the most part unrevolutionary. It must be awakened and it must be led by its natural class allies – the proletariat and the revolutionary intelligentsia.

At the top of the class structure in rural areas are the traditional feudal landlords who live on the exploitation of the peasants; and the capitalist landlords – many of whom are absentee – who are dependent on the exploitation of wage labour. Among the latter – who form part of the rural bourgeoisie – are the clergy of various sects and religions who live on the feudal and capitalist exploitation of peasants. The rural bourgeoisie own relatively large farms. They own capital, exploit wage labour, and for the most part specialise in export or 'cash' crops. The small farmers, who may be classed as petty rural bourgeoisie, possess little capital and cultivate land which they either own or rent. They employ members of their family or clan and/or wage labour. If the land is rented, the normal practice is for the petty farmer to retain about two-thirds of the proceeds of the farm himself, and to pay one-third to the owner of the land. Below the petty rural bourgeoisie in the rural strata, are the peasants, those who cultivate negligible areas of land, and are often forced to sell their labour power to become seasonal workers. Finally, there are the agricultural labourers, the rural proletariat, who own nothing but their labour.

Thus the composition of the agrarian social strata consists of two major groups – the exploiting group and the exploited. These groups can each be sub-divided into smaller groups:

The exploiting classes consist of:

a. plantation owners
b. 'absentee' landlords
c. farmers (comparatively large property owners)
d. petty farmers

The exploited classes are:

a. peasants
b. rural proletariat

The plantation owners are for the most part aliens (e.g. UAC in Nigeria, Cameroon and Zaire and white minority settlers in South Africa and Rhodesia). These plantations are extensions of monopolies in Africa. The system of exploitation here conforms to the basic law of capitalism. The farm or plantation labourers are exploited. This exploitation of African workers is made possible by the low level of the standard of living of the workers which enables the monopolies to pay low nominal wages. But due to the ever-rising prices of consumer goods, the real wages of these labourers are always declining. Hence the conflict between labour and capital is always grave. The foreign monopolies are alien absentee owners. But there also exist local absentee owners.

REVOLUTIONARY PATH (1973), pp. 341–46

The unilateral declaration of independence (UDI), by the minority government of Rhodesia on 11 November 1965, was not only the expression of racist, settler politics, but an exposure of the workings of imperialism and neocolonialism in Africa. For the settler government, representing capitalism, made it clear in UDI that the intention was to continue indefinitely, the exploitation and repression of the African people of Zimbabwe. It was the culmination of a settler policy evolved with the direct and indirect support of the British government, and of the imperialist and capitalist interest of the West.

. . . . . .

When the OAU Summit meeting took place in Accra in October 1965, the question of Rhodesia was high on the Agenda, since UDI appeared to be imminent, and Britain was apparently unprepared to deal firmly with the rebellion. The situation was made worse for us because the OAU still lacked force to implement any decisions reached. We still had no African High Command, and no unified political machinery. It was my great hope that the Accra Summit would at last set in motion the formation of an All-African High Command, and also an Executive Council as the initial step in the establishment of an All-African Union Government. But although the Rhodesian situation cried out for bold, revolutionary steps, the opportunity was missed, and instead, a series of resolutions were passed. The Assembly called on the United Nations to declare that a unilateral declaration of independence was a threat to international peace, and called for the putting into effect of all the measures necessitated by such a situation in accordance with the UN Charter to help in bringing into office a government of Rhodesia representing the majority of the people. A further resolution called on Britain to abrogate the Rhodesia constitution of 1961, and to take all necessary measures, even in the use of armed force, for the restoration of the administration of the territory, and to release political prisoners. The Assembly also called on Britain to hold a constitutional conference to be attended by representatives of all the people of Rhodesia with a view to agreeing to a new constitution ensuring the right of general elections, the right to vote and the holding of free elections. All governments and international organisations were asked to refuse recognition of the minority government in the event of UDI, and to apply sanctions against it. Further, OAU states were recommended to reconsider their political, economic, diplomatic and financial relations with Britain if Britain accepted the independence of Rhodesia on the basis of minority rule. The resolution stated that member states would use all possible means, including force, against UDI, and they would support the African people of Zimbabwe in their fight to establish majority rule in the country. They also agreed in principle on the following measures to be taken in the event of a negotiated independence:

(i) Refusal to recognise the new Rhodesian government.

(ii) Continued efforts to reconcile the two African nationalist parties – the Zimbabwe African Peoples Union and the Zimbabwe African National Union – with a view to forming a government in exile, and giving it financial, political, diplomatic and military help.

(iii) An emergency meeting of the OAU Council of Ministers to consider further action, including the most effective means of involving the United Nations.

(iv) A call to African members of the Commonwealth, and other African countries, to reconsider their relations with Britain, and bring the utmost pressure to bear on the British government; and

(v) Generally to treat Rhodesia like South Africa and the Portuguese African territories in applying such measures as an economic boycott.

A committee was formed, including Egypt, Tanzania, Kenya, Zambia and Nigeria, to follow up the resolutions of the Conference.

The futility of paper resolutions and declarations of intent without effective political and military machinery to implement them, has been amply demonstrated in the case of Rhodesia by subsequent events. The settler government declared UDI on November 1965 confident that the OAU was powerless to act, and that there would be no really meaningful pressures brought to bear by Britain or the United Nations. They were prepared for economic sanctions, and did not fear them, knowing that they would be ineffective, and that South Africa would become Rhodesia's economic support. As events proved, after some initial dislocation, the total value of Rhodesia's imports increased beyond the level attained before UDI; and as a whole, the Rhodesian economy probably suffered less than it did in the recession which accompanied the dissolution of the Federation.

. . . . .

The reactionary coup in Ghana in February 1966, greeted so jubilantly in Salisbury by the settler government, prevented follow up action. Zambia under the leadership of my good friend Kenneth Kaunda was left to bear the brunt of the continuing aggression of Smith's rebel regime. In 1971 the OAU still lacks unified political and military machinery, and the racist, minority government in Salisbury continues to defy the people of Africa who are the rightful owners of the land of Zimbabwe.

14

APPENDIX I: UDI AND NEO-COLONIALISM

UDI

The unilateral declaration of independence (UDI), by the minority government of Rhodesia on 11 November 1965, was not only the expression of racist, settler politics, but an exposure of the workings of imperialism and neocolonialism in Africa. For the settler government, representing capitalism, made it clear in UDI that the intention was to continue indefinitely, the exploitation and repression of the African people of Zimbabwe. It was the culmination of a settler policy evolved with the direct and indirect support of the British government, and of the imperialist and capitalist interests of the West.

NEO-COLONIALISM

My purpose in writing *Neo-Colonialism: The Last Stage of Imperialism* was to expose the workings of international monopoly capitalism in Africa in order to show the meaninglessness of political freedom without economic independence, and to demonstrate the urgent need for the unification of Africa and a socialist transformation of society.

The US State Department reacted sharply to the publication of the book, and in an Aide Memoire protested particularly against Chapter 18 where I drew attention to the activities in Africa of the Peace Corps, the US Information Services, the US Agency for International Development, and to the World Bank. The State Department considered the book 'anti-American in tone', though it was neocolonialist practices and not governments which were attacked in the book.

The State Department followed up its protest with the rejection of a request from my government for 35 million dollars' worth of surplus food shipments. A headline in the *New York Herald Tribune* of Wednesday, 24th November, 1965 declared: 'Ghana Bites US hand so Feeding is Halted'. The State Department protest was conveyed orally by Mennen Williams, the Assistant Secretary of State for African Affairs, in a meeting with Miguel Augustus Ribeiro, the Ghanaian ambassador to the USA. The rejection of the food-for-peace aid request followed two days later.

The text of the US Aide Memoire delivered by Mennen Williams to Ribeiro on 18 November 1965 was contained in a telegram from Ribeiro to the Ministry of Foreign Affairs in Accra. It read as follows:

> I refer to my cyphered message WA/484 of 2nd November on American reaction to Osagyefo's latest book 'Neo-Colonialism'.
> At 12.30 this afternoon Governor Mennen Williams, on behalf of the United States Government, handed me a formal Aide-Memoire protesting against alleged attacks by Osagyefo on the (United States) in (public). I quote below the text of the protest:
> 'The United States has noted with profound alarm the attacks against the United States in President Nkrumah's book, *Neo-Colonialism: The Last Stage of Imperialism*. This represents an unprecedented attack by the Head of State of a friendly country against the United States, a country which has by word and deed shown repeatedly over the years its desire to maintain friendly relations with the people and government of Ghana.

The book appears to have been designed for the specific purpose of creating in the minds of its readers suspicion and distrust of the motives, intentions and actions of the United States. The hostility of the book exhibits, particularly in Chapter 18, and its general provocation and anti-American tone, are deeply disturbing and offensive to the Government's goodwill.

The Government of the United States actually therefore holds the Government of Ghana fully responsible for whatever consequences the book's publication may have.'

Before handing in the protest Mr Mennen Williams expressed his personal disappointment and that of his government at the attacks on the United States which are considered by them to be very hostile.

I explained that nothing had been stated in the book which had not been said before even by American writers as evidenced by the profuse quotations from the book entitled 'Invisible Government' and that (far from) sharp sentences intending to attack the United States, it could be inferred from arguments and conclusions in the book that Osagyefo's real intention was to point out to his fellow African leaders the dangers that disunity exposes them to, and the need for the formation of a Union Government of Africa. I assured him also of Osagyefo's high regard for the person of President Johnson and pointed out that neither from books created from Osagyefo's past record could anyone justifiably accuse Osagyefo of indulging in personal attacks on heads of Governments even though some other heads of Governments had from time to time attacked Osagyefo personally. I emphasised that what Osagyefo has attacked is a system and not the American President and Government. Needless to say, Governor Williams was not convinced.

I was given the impression that the protest may not be the last word of the issue. I advise that the protest be taken seriously and an appropriate reply be sent at an early date through me or the United States Charge d'Affaires and copied to me.'

According to an article which appeared in the *Baltimore Sun* on 23 November 1965, State department officials denied that the rejection of Ghana's request for food-for-peace aid was directly connected with the publication of *Neo-Colonialism*. But they did not deny that relations between the USA and Ghana had reached 'a new low as a result of Nkrumah's charges that the United States is foremost among the neocolonialist powers seeking to exploit and subjugate the African continent'. What appeared to annoy the State Department was the timing of the publication, and the fact that copies of the book were circulated among the African heads of state and their delegations attending the OAU Summit meeting in Accra in October 1965.

Neocolonialism is a stage in the development of imperialism. In the sub-title of my book I refer to it as the 'last stage' since I considered it the last thrust of imperialism before the ultimate and inevitable victory of the masses over all forms of oppression and exploitation. The 'last stage' may be said to have developed with full force after the Second World War, in 1945. Before then, neocolonialism had reared its head in Latin America and elsewhere, though it was not until after the Second World War that neocolonialism became the predominant expression of imperialism.

Neocolonialism is more insidious, complex and dangerous than the old colonialism. It not only prevents its victims from developing their economic potential for their own use, but it controls the political life of the country, and supports the indigenous bourgeoisie in perpetuating the oppression and exploitation of the masses. Under neocolonialism, the economic systems and political policies of independent territories are managed and manipulated from outside, by international monopoly finance capital in league with the indigenous bourgeoisie.

The policy of balkanisation pursued by the imperialist powers when forced to concede political independence in Asia, Africa and Latin America, reflects the strategy of neocolonialism – the intention being to ensure their continued exploitation and oppression.

UDI AND NEO-COLONIALISM

In Africa, most of the independent states are economically unviable, and still have the artificial frontiers of colonialism. They are easy prey for the voracious appetites of neo-colonialist empire builders. Where political balkanisation has not been successful for the imperialists, economic balkanisation has been pursued. A single productive process is divided between states. Communications, banking, insurance, and other key services are controlled by neocolonialists. Then regional economic groupings in Africa have been encouraged, controlled by neocolonialists, which therefore further strengthen international finance capital. Backing up these processes, the power of international monopoly finance is used to force down the price of raw materials, and to keep up the price of foreign manufactured goods.

In recent times, a further tactic of neocolonialism is to appear to support liberation movements, and even to give donations to them, where such movements are thought to be the expression of bourgeois nationalism, and not the outcome of genuine socialist revolutionary effort. For the ending of direct colonial rule and the emergence of a puppet government facilitates neocolonialism by opening the door to exploitation from a wider range of neocolonialists than those represented by a single former colonial power. By concentrating on political struggles to end direct colonial rule, or to force minority regimes to grant reforms, attention is diverted from economic and domestic issues, and the insidious processes of neocolonialism can proceed. Meanwhile, many of the puppet rulers of Africa masquerade as 'revolutionaries' and 'liberators', and serve the interest of their neocolonialist masters by trying to mask the reactionary nature of their regimes.

It is very significant, that of all my books, *Neo-Colonialism* is the only one which has caused a government to register a formal protest.

EXTRACTS FROM *NEO-COLONIALISM: THE LAST STAGE OF IMPERIALISM*

INTRODUCTION

The neo-colonialism of today represents imperialism in its final and perhaps its most dangerous stage. In the past it was possible to convert a country upon which a neo-colonial regime had been imposed – Egypt in the nineteenth century is an example – into a colonial territory. Today this process is no longer feasible. Old-fashioned colonialism is by no means entirely abolished. It still constitutes an African problem, but it is everywhere on the retreat. Once a territory has become nominally independent it is no longer possible, as it was in the last century, to reverse the process. Existing colonies may linger on, but no new colonies will be created. In place of colonialism as the main instrument of imperialism we have today neo-colonialism.

The essence of neo-colonialism is that the State which is subject to it is, in theory, independent and has all the outward trappings of international sovereignty. In reality its economic system and thus its political policy is directed from outside.

The methods and form of this direction can take various shapes. For example, in an extreme case the troops of the imperial power may garrison the territory of the neo-colonial State and control the government of it. More often, however, neo-colonialist control is exercised through economic or monetary means. The neo-colonial State may be obliged to take the manufactured products of the imperialist power to the exclusion of competing products from elsewhere. Control over government policy in the neo-colonial State may be secured by payments towards the cost of running the State, by the provision of civil servants in positions where they can dictate policy and by monetary control over foreign exchange through the imposition of a banking system controlled by the imperial power.

Where neo-colonialism exists the power exercising control is often the State which formerly ruled the territory in question, but this is not necessarily so. For example, in the case of South Vietnam the former imperial power was France, but neo-colonial control of the State has now gone to the United States. It is possible that neo-colonial control may be exercised by a consortium of financial interests which are not specifically identifiable with any particular State. The control of the Congo by great international financial concerns is a case in point.

UDI AND NEO-COLONIALISM

The result of neo-colonialism is that foreign capital is used for the exploitation rather than for the development of the less developed parts of the world. Investment under neo-colonialism increases rather than decreases the gap between the rich and the poor countries of the world. The struggle against neo-colonialism is not aimed at excluding the capital of the developed world from operating in less developed countries. It is aimed at preventing the financial power of the developed countries being used in such a way as to impoverish the less developed.

Non-alignment, as practised by Ghana and many other countries, is based on co-operation with all States whether they be capitalist, socialist or have a mixed economy. Such a policy, therefore, involves foreign investment from capitalist countries, but it must be invested in accordance with a national plan drawn up by the government of the non-aligned State with its own interests in mind. The issue is not what return the foreign investor receives on his investments. He may, in fact, do better for himself if he invests in a non-aligned country than if he invests in a neo-colonial one. The question is one of power. A State in the grip of neo-colonialism is not master of its own destiny. It is this factor which makes neo-colonialism such a serious threat to world peace. The growth of nuclear weapons has made out of date the old-fashioned balance of power which rested upon the ultimate sanction of a major war. Certainty of mutual mass destruction effectively prevents either of the great power blocs from threatening the other with the possibility of a world-wide war, and military conflict has thus become confined to 'limited wars'. For these neo-colonialism is the breeding ground.

Such wars can, of course take place in countries which are not neo-colonialist controlled. Indeed their object may be to establish in a small but independent country a neo-colonialist regime. The evil of neo-colonialism is that it prevents the formation of those large units which would make impossible 'limited war'. To give one example: if Africa was united, no major power bloc would attempt to subdue it by limited war because from the very nature of limited war, what can be achieved by it is itself limited. It is only where small States exist that it is possible, by landing a few thousand marines or by financing a mercenary force, to secure a decisive result.

The restriction of military action of 'limited wars' is, however, no guarantee of world peace and is likely to be the factor which will ultimately involve the great power blocs in a world war, however much both are determined to avoid it.

Limited war, once embarked upon, achieves a momentum of its own. Of this, the war in South Vietnam is only one example. It escalates despite the desire of the great power blocs to keep it limited. While this particular war may be prevented from leading to a world conflict, the multiplication of similar limited wars can only have one end – world war and the terrible consequences of nuclear conflict.

Neo-colonialism is also the worst form of imperialism. For those who practise it, it means power without responsibility and for those who suffer from it, it means exploitation without redress. In the days of old-fashioned colonialism, the imperial power had at least to explain and justify at home the actions it was taking abroad. In the colony those who served the ruling imperial power could at least look to its protection against any violent move by their opponents. With neo-colonialism neither is the case.

Above all, neo-colonialism, like colonialism before it, postpones the facing of the social issues which will have to be faced by the fully developed sector of the world before the danger of world war can be eliminated or the problem of world poverty resolved.

Neo-colonialism, like colonialism, is an attempt to export the social conflicts of the capitalist countries. The temporary success of this policy can be seen in the ever widening gap between the richer and the poorer nations of the world. But the internal contradictions and conflicts of neo-colonialism make it certain that it cannot endure as a permanent world policy. How it should be brought to an end is a problem that should be studied, above all, by the developed nations of the world, because it is they who will feel the full impact of the ultimate failure. The longer it continues the more certain it is that its inevitable collapse will destroy the social system of which they had made it a foundation.

The reason for its development in the post-war period can be briefly summarized. The problem which faced the wealthy nations of the world at the end of the second world war was the impossibility of returning to the pre-war situation in which there was a great gulf between the few rich and the many poor. Irrespective of what particular political party was in power, the internal pressures in the rich countries of the world were such that no post-war capitalist country could survive unless it became a 'Welfare State'. There might be differences in degree in the extent of the social benefits given to the industrial and agricultural workers, but what was everywhere impossible was a return to the mass unemployment and to the low level of living of the pre-war years.

From the end of the nineteenth century onwards, colonies had been regarded as a source of wealth which could be used to mitigate the class conflicts in the capitalist States and, as will be explained later, this policy had some success. But it failed in its ultimate object because the pre-war capitalist States were so organized internally that the bulk of the profit made from colonial possessions found its way into the pockets of the capitalist class and not into those of the workers. Far from achieving the object intended, the working class parties at times tended to identify their interests with those of the colonial peoples and the imperialist powers found themselves engaged upon a conflict on two fronts, at home with their own workers and abroad against the growing forces of colonial liberation.

The post-war period inaugurated a very different colonial policy. A deliberate attempt was made to divert colonial earnings from the wealthy class and use them instead generally to finance the 'Welfare State'. As will be seen from the examples given later, this was a method consciously adopted even by those working-class leaders who had before the war regarded the colonial peoples as their natural allies against their capitalist enemies at home.

At first it was presumed that this object could be achieved by maintaining the pre-war colonial system. Experience soon proved that attempts to do so would be disastrous and would only provoke colonial wars, thus dissipating the anticipated gains from the continuance of the colonial regime. Britain, in particular, realized this at an early stage and the correctness of the British judgement at the time has subsequently been demonstrated by the defeat of French colonialism in the Far East and Algeria and the failure of the Dutch to retain any of their former colonial empire.

The system of neo-colonialism was therefore instituted and in the short run it has served the developed powers admirably. It is in the long run that its consequences are likely to be catastrophic for them.

Neo-colonialism is based upon the principle of breaking up former large united colonial territories into a number of small non-viable States which are incapable of independent development and must rely upon the former imperial power for defence and even internal security. Their economic and financial systems are linked, as in colonial days, with those of the former colonial ruler.

At first sight the scheme would appear to have many advantages for the developed countries of the world. All the profits of neo-colonialism can be secured if, in any given area, a reasonable proportion of the States have a neo-colonialist system. It is not necessary that they *all* should have one. Unless small States can combine they must be compelled to sell their primary products at prices dictated by the developed nations and buy their manufactured goods at the prices fixed by them. So long as neo-colonialism can prevent political and economic conditions for optimum development, the developing countries, whether they are under neo-colonialist control or not, will be unable to create a large enough market to support industrialization. In the same way they will lack the financial strength to force the developed countries to accept their primary products at a fair price.

In the neo-colonialist territories, since the former colonial power has in theory relinquished political control, if the social conditions occasioned by neo-colonialism cause a revolt the loyal neo-colonialist government can be sacrificed and another equally subservient one substituted in its place. On the other hand, in any continent where neo-colonialism exists on a wide scale the same social pressures which can produce revolts in neo-colonial territories will also affect those States which have refused to accept the system and therefore neo-colonialist nations have a ready-made weapon with which they can threaten their opponents if they appear successfully to be challenging the system.

These advantages, which seem at first sight so obvious, are, however, on examination, illusory because they fail to take into consideration the facts of the world today.

The introduction of neo-colonialism increases the rivalry between the great powers which was provoked by the old-style colonialism. However little real power the government of a neo-colonialist State may possess, it must have, from the very fact of its nominal independence, a certain area of manoeuvre. It may not be able to exist without a neo-colonialist master but it may still have the ability to change masters.

The ideal neo-colonialist State would be one which was wholly subservient to neo-colonialist interests but the existence of the socialist nations makes it impossible to enforce the full rigour of the neo-colonialist system. The existence of an alternative system is itself a challenge to the neo-colonialist regime. Warnings about 'the dangers of Communist subversion' are likely to be two-edged since they bring to the notice of those living under a neo-colonialist system the possibility of a change of regime. In fact neo-colonialism is the victim of its own contradictions. In order to make it attractive to those upon whom it is practised it must be shown as capable of raising their living standards, but the economic object of neo-colonialism is to keep those standards depressed in the interest of the developed countries. It is only when this contradiction is understood that the failure of innumerable 'aid' programmes, many of them well intentioned, can be explained.

In the first place, the rulers of neo-colonial States derive their authority to govern, not from the will of the people, but from the support which they obtain from their neo-colonialist masters. They have therefore little interest in developing education, strengthening the bargaining power of their workers employed by expatriate firms, or indeed of taking any step which would challenge the colonial pattern of commerce and industry, which it is the object of neo-colonialism to preserve. 'Aid', therefore, to a neo-colonial State is merely a revolving credit, paid by the neo-colonial master, passing through the neo-colonial State and returning to the neo-colonial master in the form of increased profits.

Secondly, it is in the field of 'aid' that the rivalry of individual developed States first manifests itself. So long as neo-colonialism persists so long will spheres of interest persist, and this makes multilateral aid – which is in fact the only effective form of aid – impossible.

Once multilateral aid begins the neo-colonialist masters are faced by the hostility of the vested interests in their own country. Their manufacturers naturally object to any attempt to raise the price of the raw materials which they obtain from the neo-colonialist territory in question, or to the establishment there of manufacturing industries which might compete directly or indirectly with their own exports to the territory. Even education is suspect as likely to produce a student movement and it is, of course, true that in many less developed countries the students have been in the vanguard of the fight against neo-colonialism.

In the end the situation arises that the only type of aid which the neo-colonialist masters consider as safe is 'military aid'.

Once a neo-colonialist territory is brought to such a state of economic chaos and misery that revolt actually breaks out then, and only then, is there no limit to the generosity of the neo-colonial overlord, provided, of course, that the funds supplied are utilized exclusively for military purposes.

Military aid in fact marks the last stage of neo-colonialism and its effect is self-destructive. Sooner or later the weapons supplied pass into the hands of the opponents of the neo-colonialist regime and the war itself increases the social misery which originally provoked it.

Neo-colonialism is a mill-stone around the necks of the developed countries which practise it. Unless they can rid themselves of it, it will drown them. Previously the developed powers could escape from the contradictions of neo-colonialism by substituting for it direct colonialism.

Such a solution is no longer possible and the reasons for it have been well explained by Mr Owen Lattimore, the United States Far Eastern expert and adviser to Chiang Kai-shek in the immediate post-war period. He wrote:

> 'Asia, which was so easily and swiftly subjugated by conquerors in the eighteenth and nineteenth centuries, displayed an amazing ability stubbornly to resist modern armies equipped with aeroplanes, tanks, motor vehicles and mobile artillery.
>
> Formerly big territories were conquered in Asia with small forces. Income, first of all from plunder, then from direct taxes and lastly from trade, capital investments and long-term exploitation, covered with incredible speed the expenditure for military operations. This arithmetic represented a great temptation to strong countries. Now they have run up against another arithmetic, and it discourages them.'

The same arithmetic is likely to apply throughout the less developed world.

This book is therefore an attempt to examine neo-colonialism not only in its African context and its relation to African unity, but in world perspective. Neo-colonialism is by no means exclusively an African question. Long before it was practised on any large scale in Africa it was an established system in other parts of the world. Nowhere has it proved successful, either in raising living standards or in ultimately benefiting the countries which have indulged in it.

Marx predicted that the growing gap between the wealth of the possessing classes and the workers it employs would ultimately produce a conflict fatal to capitalism in each individual capitalist State.

This conflict between the rich and the poor has now been transferred on to the international scene, but for proof of what is acknowledged to be happening it is no longer necessary to consult the classical Marxist writers. The situation is set out with the utmost clarity in the leading organs of capitalist opinion. Take for example the following extracts from *The Wall Street Journal*, the newspaper which perhaps best reflects United States capitalist thinking.

In its issue of 12th May, 1965, under the headline of 'Poor Nations' Plight', the paper first analyses 'which countries are considered industrial and which backward'. There is, it explains, 'no rigid method of classification'. Nevertheless, it points out:

> 'A generally used breakdown, however, has recently been maintained by the International Monetary Fund because, in the words of an IMF official,

UDI AND NEO-COLONIALISM

"the economic demarcation in the world is getting increasingly apparent". The breakdown, the official says, "is based on simple common sense".

In the IMF's view, the industrial counties are the United States, the United Kingdom, most West European nations, Canada and Japan. A special category called "other developed areas" includes such other European lands as Finland, Greece and Ireland, plus Australia, New Zealand and South Africa. The IMF's "less developed" category embraces all of Latin America and nearly all of the Middle East, non-Communist Asia and Africa.'

In other words the 'backward' countries are those situated in the neo-colonial areas.

After quoting figures to support its argument, *The Wall Street Journal* comments on this situation:

'The industrial nations have added nearly $2 billion to their reserves, which now approximate $52 billion. At the same time, the reserves of the less-developed group not only have stopped rising, but have declined some $200 million. To analysts such as Britain's Miss Ward, the significance of such statistics is clear: the economic gap is rapidly widening "between a white, complacent, highly bourgeois, very wealthy, very small North Atlantic elite and everybody else, and this is not a very comfortable heritage to leave to one's children".

"Everybody else" includes approximately two-thirds of the population of the earth, spread through about 100 nations.'

This is no new problem. In the opening paragraph of his book, *The War on World Poverty*, written in 1953, the present British Labour leader, Mr Harold Wilson, summarized the major problem of the world as he then saw it:

'For the vast majority of mankind the most urgent problem is not war, or Communism, or the cost of living, or taxation. It is hunger. Over 1,500,000,000 people, something like two-thirds of the world's population, are living in conditions of acute hunger, defined in terms of identifiable nutritional disease. This hunger is at the same time the effect and the cause of the poverty, squalor and misery in which they live.'

Its consequences are likewise understood. The correspondent of *The Wall Street Journal*, previously quoted, underlines them:

'... many diplomats and economists view the implications as overwhelmingly – and dangerously – political. Unless the present decline can be reversed, these analysts fear, the United States and other wealthy industrial powers of the West face the distinct possibility, in the words of British economist Barbara Ward, "of a sort of international class war".'

What is lacking are any positive proposals for dealing with the situation. All that *The Wall Street Journal*'s correspondent can do is to point out that the traditional methods recommended for curing the evils are only likely to make the situation worse.

It has been argued that the developed nations should effectively assist the poorer parts of the world, and that the whole world should be turned into a Welfare State. However, there seems little prospect that anything of this sort could be achieved. The so-called 'aid' programmes to help backward economies represent, according to a rough UN estimate, only one half of one per cent of the total income of industrial countries. But when it comes to the prospect of increasing such aid the mood is one of pessimism:

> 'A large school of thought holds that expanded share-the-wealth schemes are idealistic and impractical. This school contends climate, undeveloped human skills, lack of natural resources and other factors – not just lack of money – retard economic progress in many of these lands, and that the countries lack personnel with the training or will to use vastly expanded aid effectively. Share-the-wealth schemes, according to this view, would be like pouring money down a bottomless well, weakening the donor nations without effectively curing the ills of the recipients.'

The absurdity of this argument is demonstrated by the fact that every one of the reasons quoted to prove why the less developed parts of the world cannot be developed applied equally strongly to the present developed countries in the period prior to their development. The argument is only true in this sense. The less developed world will not become developed through the goodwill or generosity of the developed powers. It can only become developed through a struggle against the external forces which have a vested interest in keeping it undeveloped.

Of these forces, neo-colonialism is, at this stage of history, the principal.

I propose to analyse neo-colonialism, first, by examining the state of the African continent and showing how neo-colonialism at the moment keeps it artificially poor. Next, I propose to show how in practice African Unity, which in itself can only be established by the defeat of neo-colonialism, could immensely raise African living standards. From this beginning, I propose to examine neo-colonialism generally, first historically and then by a consideration of the great international monopolies whose continued stranglehold on the neo-colonial sectors of the world ensures the continuation of the system.

UDI AND NEO-COLONIALISM

THE MECHANISMS OF NEO-COLONIALISM

In order to halt foreign interference in the affairs of developing countries it is necessary to study, understand, expose and actively combat neo-colonialism in whatever guise it may appear. For the methods of neo-colonialists are subtle and varied. They operate not only in the economic field, but also in the political, religious, ideological and cultural spheres.

Faced with the militant peoples of the ex-colonial territories in Asia, Africa, the Caribbean and Latin America, imperialism simply switches tactics. Without a qualm it dispenses with its flags, and even with certain of its more hated expatriate officials. This means, so it claims, that it is 'giving' independence to its former subjects, to be followed by 'aid' for their development. Under cover of such phrases, however, it devises innumerable ways to accomplish objectives formerly achieved by naked colonialism. It is this sum total of these modern attempts to perpetuate colonialism while at the same time talking about 'freedom', which has come to be known as *neo-colonialism*.

Foremost among the neo-colonialists is the United States, which has long exercised its power in Latin America. Fumblingly at first she turned towards Europe, and then with more certainty after world war two when most countries of that continent were indebted to her. Since then, with methodical thoroughness and touching attention to detail, the Pentagon set about consolidating its ascendancy, evidence of which can be seen all around the world.

Who really rules in such places as Great Britain, West Germany, Japan, Spain, Portugal or Italy? If General de Gaulle is 'defecting' from US monopoly control, what interpretation can be placed on his 'experiments' in the Sahara desert, his paratroopers in Gabon, or his trips to Cambodia and Latin America?

Lurking behind such questions are the extended tentacles of the Wall Street octopus. And its suction cups and muscular strength are provided by a phenomenon dubbed 'The Invisible Government', arising from Wall Street's connection with the Pentagon and various intelligence services. I quote:

> 'The Invisible Government... is a loose amorphous grouping of individuals and agencies drawn from many parts of the visible government. It is not limited to the Central Intelligence Agency, although the CIA is at its heart. Nor is it confined to the nine other agencies which comprise what is known as the intelligence community: the National Security Council, the Defense

Intelligence Agency, the National Security Agency, Army Intelligence, Navy Intelligence and Research, the Atomic Energy Commission and the Federal Bureau of Investigation.

The Invisible Government includes also many other units and agencies, as well as individuals, that appear outwardly to be a normal part of the conventional government. It even encompasses business firms and institutions that are seemingly private.

To an extent that is only beginning to be perceived, this shadow government is shaping the lives of 190,000,000 Americans. An informed citizen might come to suspect that the foreign policy of the United States often works publicly in one direction and secretly through the Invisible Government in just the opposite direction.

This Invisible Government is a relatively new institution. It came into being as a result of two related factors: the rise of the United States after World War II to a position of pre-eminent world power, and the challenge to that power by Soviet Communism....

By 1964 the intelligence network had grown into a massive hidden apparatus, secretly employing about 200,000 persons and spending billions of dollars a year.'*

Here, from the very citadel of neo-colonialism, is a description of the apparatus which now directs all other Western intelligence set-ups either by persuasion or by force. Results were achieved in Algeria during the April 1961 plot of anti-de Gaulle generals; as also in Guatemala, Iraq, Iran, Suez and the famous U-2 spy intrusion of Soviet air space which wrecked the approaching Summit, then in West Germany and again in East Germany in the riots of 1953, in Hungary's abortive crisis of 1959, Poland's of September 1956, and in Korea, Burma, Formosa, Laos, Cambodia and South Vietnam; they are evident in the trouble in Congo (Leopoldville) which began with Lumumba's murder, and continues till now; in events in Cuba, Turkey, Cyprus, Greece, and in other places too numerous to catalogue completely.

And with what aim have these innumerable incidents occurred? The general objective has been mentioned: to achieve colonialism in fact while preaching independence.

On the economic front, a strong factor favouring Western monopolies and acting against the developing world is international capital's control of the world market, as well as of the prices of commodities bought and sold there. From 1951 to 1961, without taking oil into consideration, the

---

* *The Invisible Government*, David Wise and Thomas B. Ross, Random House, New York, 1964.

general level of prices for primary products fell by 33.1 per cent, while prices of manufactured goods rose 3.5 per cent (within which, machinery and equipment prices rose 31.3 per cent). In that same decade this caused a loss to the Asian, African and Latin American countries, using 1951 prices as a basis, of some $41,400 million. In the same period, while the volume of exports from these countries rose, their earnings in foreign exchange from such exports decreased.

Another technique of neo-colonialism is the use of high rates of interest. Figures from the World Bank for 1962 showed that seventy-one Asian, African and Latin American countries owed foreign debts of some $27,000 million, on which they paid in interest and service charges some $5,000 million. Since then, such foreign debts have been estimated as more than £30,000 million in these areas. In 1961, the interest rates on almost three-quarters of the loans offered by the major imperialist powers amounted to more than five per cent, in some cases up to seven or eight per cent, while the call-in periods of such loans have been burdensomely short.

While capital worth $30,000 million was exported to some fifty-six developing countries between 1956 and 1962, it is estimated this interest and profit alone extracted on this sum from the debtor countries amounted to more than £15,000 million. This method of penetration by economic aid recently soared into prominence when a number of countries began rejecting it. Ceylon, Indonesia and Cambodia are among those who turned it down. Such 'aid' is estimated on the annual average to have amounted to $2,600 million between 1951 and 1955; $4,007 million between 1956 and 1959, and $6,000 million between 1960 and 1962. But the average sums taken out of the aided countries by such donors in a sample year, 1961, are estimated to amount to $5,000 million, in profits, $1,000 million in interest, and $5,800 million from non-equivalent exchange, or a total of $11,800 million extracted against $6,000 million put in. Thus, 'aid' turns out to be another means of exploitation, a modern method of capital export under a more cosmetic name.

Still another neo-colonialist trap on the economic front has come to be known as 'multilateral aid' through international organizations: the International Monetary Fund, the International Bank for Reconstruction and Development (known as the World Bank), the International Finance Corporation and the International Development Association are examples, all, significantly, having US capital as their major backing. These agencies have the habit of forcing would-be borrowers to submit to various offensive conditions, such as supplying information about their economies, submitting their policy and plans to review by the World Bank and accepting agency supervision of their use of loans. As for the alleged development, between 1960 and mid-1963 the International Development Association promised a total of $500 million to applicants, out of which only $70 million were actually received.

In more recent years, as pointed out by Monitor in *The Times*, 1st July, 1965, there has been a substantial increase in communist technical and economic aid activities in developing countries. During 1964 the total amount of assistance offered was approximately £600 million. This was almost a third of the total communist aid given during the previous decade. The Middle East received about 40 per cent of the total, Asia 36 per cent, Africa 22 per cent and Latin America the rest.

Increased Chinese activity was responsible to some extent for the larger amount of aid offered in 1964, though China contributed only a quarter of the total aid committed; the Soviet Union provided a half, and the East European countries a quarter.

Although aid from socialist countries still falls far short of that offered from the west, it is often more impressive, since it is swift and flexible, and interest rates on communist loans are only about two per cent compared with five to six per cent charged on loans from western countries.

Nor is the whole story of 'aid' contained in figures, for there are conditions which hedge it around: the conclusion of commerce and navigation treaties; agreements for economic co-operation; the right to meddle in internal finances, including currency and foreign exchange, to lower trade barriers in favour of the donor country's goods and capital; to protect the interests of private investments; determination of how the funds are to be used; forcing the recipient to set up counterpart funds; to supply raw materials to the donor; and use of such funds – a majority of it, in fact – to buy goods from the donor nation. These conditions apply to industry, commerce, agriculture, shipping and insurance, apart from others which are political and military.

So-called 'invisible trade' furnished the Western monopolies with yet another means of economic penetration. Over 90 per cent of world ocean shipping is controlled by the imperialist countries. They control shipping rates and, between 1951 and 1961, they increased them some five times in a total rise of about 60 per cent, the upward trend continuing. Thus, net annual freight expenses incurred by Asia, Africa and Latin America amount to no less than an estimated $1,600 million. This is over and above all other profits and interest payments. As for insurance payments, in 1961 alone these amounted to an unfavourable balance in Asia, Africa and Latin America of some additional $370 million.

Having waded through all this, however, we have begun to understand only the *basic* methods of neo-colonialism. The full extent of its inventiveness is far from exhausted.

In the labour field, for example, imperialism operates through labour arms like the Social Democratic parties of Europe led by the British Labour Party, and through such instruments as the International Confederation of Free Trade Unions (ICFTU), now apparently being superseded by the New York Africa-American Labor Centre (AALC) under AFL-CIO chief George Meany and the well-known CIA man in labour's top echelons, Irving Brown.

In 1945, out of the euphoria of anti-fascist victory, the World Federation of Trade Unions (WFTU) had been formed, including all world labour except the US American Federation of Labor (AFL). By 1949, however, led by the British Trade Union Congress (TUC), a number of pro-imperialist labour bodies in the West broke away from the WFTU over the issue of anti-colonialist liberation, and set up the ICFTU.

For ten years it continued under British TUC leadership. Its record in Africa, Asia and Latin America could gratify only the big international monopolies which were extracting super-profits from those areas.

In 1959, at Brussels, the United States AFL-CIO union centre fought for and won control of the ICFTU Executive Board. From then on a flood of typewriters, mimeograph machines, cars, supplies, buildings, salaries and, so it is still averred, outright bribes for labour leaders in various parts of the developing world rapidly linked ICFTU in the minds of the rank and file with the CIA. To such an extent did its prestige suffer under these American bosses that, in 1964, the AFL-CIO brains felt it necessary to establish a fresh outfit. They set up the AALC in New York right across the river from the United Nations.

'As a steadfast champion of national independence, democracy and social justice', unblushingly stated the April 1965 Bulletin put out by this Centre, 'the AFL-CIO will strengthen its efforts to assist the advancement of the economic conditions of the African peoples. Toward this end, steps have been taken to expand assistance to the African free trade unions by organizing the African-American Labour Centre. Such assistance will help African labour play a vital role in the economic and democratic upbuilding of their countries.'

The March issue of this Bulletin, however, gave the game away: 'In mobilizing capital resources for investment in Workers Education, Vocational Training, Co-operatives, Health Clinics and Housing, the Centre will work with both private and public institutions. It will also *encourage labour-management co-operation to expand American capital investment in the African nations.*' The italics are mine. Could anything be plainer?

Following a pattern previously set by the ICFTU, it has already started classes: one for drivers and mechanics in Nigeria, one in tailoring in Kenya. Labour scholarships are being offered to Africans who want to study trade unionism in – of all places – Austria, ostensibly by the Austrian unions. Elsewhere, labour, organized into political parties of which the British Labour Party is a leading and typical example has shown a similar aptitude for encouraging 'Labour-management co-operation to expand ... capital investment in African nations.'

But as the struggle sharpens, even these measures of neo-colonialism are proving too mild. So Africa, Asia and Latin America have begun to experience a round of coups d'état or would-be coups, together with a series of political assassinations which have destroyed in their political primes some of the newly emerging nations' best leaders. To ensure success in these endeavours, the imperialists have made widespread and wily use of ideological and cultural weapons in the form of intrigues, manoeuvres and slander campaigns.

Some of these methods used by neo-colonialists to slip past our guard must now be examined. The first is retention by the departing colonialists of various kinds of privileges which infringe on our sovereignty: that of setting up military bases or stationing troops in former colonies and the supplying of 'advisers' of one sort or another. Sometimes a number of 'rights' are demanded: land concessions, prospecting rights for minerals and/or oil; the 'right' to collect customs, to carry out administration, to issue paper money; to be exempt from customs duties and/or taxes for expatriate enterprises; and, above all, the 'right' to provide 'aid'. Also demanded and granted are privileges in the cultural field; that Western information services be exclusive; and that those from socialist countries be excluded.

Even the cinema stories of fabulous Hollywood are loaded. One has only to listen to the cheers of an African audience as Hollywood's heroes slaughter Red Indians or Asiatics to understand the effectiveness of this weapon. For, in the developing continents, where the colonialist heritage has left a vast majority still illiterate, even the smallest child gets the message contained in the blood and thunder stories emanating from California. And along with murder and the Wild West goes an incessant barrage of anti-socialist propaganda, in which the trade union man, the revolutionary, or the man of dark skin is generally cast as the villain, while the policeman, the gumshoe, the Federal agent – in a word, the CIA-type spy – is ever the hero. Here, truly, is the ideological under-belly of those political murders which so often use local people as their instruments.

While Hollywood takes care of fiction, the enormous monopoly press, together with the outflow of slick, clever, expensive magazines, attends to what it chooses to call 'news'. Within separate countries, one or two news agencies control the news handouts, so that a deadly uniformity is achieved, regardless of the number of separate newspapers or magazines; while internationally, the financial preponderance of the United States is felt more and more through its foreign correspondents and offices abroad, as well as through its influence over international capitalist journalism. Under this guise, a flood of anti-liberation propaganda emanates from the capital cities of the West, directed against China, Vietnam Indonesia, Algeria, Ghana and all countries which hack out their own independent path to freedom. Prejudice is rife. For example, wherever there is armed struggle against the forces of reaction, the nationalists are referred to as rebels, terrorists, or frequently 'communist terrorists'!

Perhaps one of the most insidious methods of the neo-colonialists is evangelism. Following the liberation movement there has been a veritable riptide of religious sects, the overwhelming majority of them American. Typical of these are Jehovah's Witnesses who recently created trouble in certain developing countries by busily teaching their citizens not to salute the new national flags. 'Religion' was too thin to smother the outcry that arose against this activity, and a temporary lull followed. But the number of evangelists continues to grow.

Yet even evangelism and the cinema are only two twigs on a much bigger tree. Dating from the end of 1961, the US has actively developed a huge ideological plan for invading the so-called Third World, utilizing all its facilities from press and radio to Peace Corps.

During 1962 and 1963 a number of international conferences to this end were held in several places, such as Nicosia in Cyprus, San José in Costa Rica, and Lagos in Nigeria. Participants, included the CIA, the US Information Agency (USIA), the Pentagon, the International Development Agency, the Peace Corps and others. Programmes were drawn up which included the systematic use of US citizens abroad in virtual intelligence activities and propaganda work. Methods of recruiting political agents and of forcing 'alliances' with the USA were worked out. At the centre of its programmes lay the demand for an absolute US monopoly in the field of propaganda, as well as for counteracting any independent efforts by developing states in the realm of information.

The United States sought, and still seeks, with considerable success, to co-ordinate on the basis of its own strategy the propaganda activities of all Western countries. In October 1961, a conference of NATO countries was held in Rome to discuss problems of psychological warfare. It appealed for the organization of combined ideological operations in Afro-Asian countries by all participants.

In May and June 1962 a seminar was convened by the US in Vienna on ideological warfare. It adopted a secret decision to engage in a propaganda offensive against the developing countries along lines laid down by the USA. It was agreed that NATO propaganda agencies would, in practice if not in the public eye, keep in close contact with US Embassies in their respective countries.

Among instruments of such Western psychological warfare are numbered the intelligence agencies of Western countries headed by those of the United States 'Invisible Government'. But most significant among them all are Moral Re-Armament (MRA), the Peace Corps and the United States Information Agency (USIA).

Moral Re-Armament is an organization founded in 1938 by the American, Frank Buchman. In the last days before the second world war, it advocated the appeasement of Hitler, often extolling Himmler, the Gestapo chief. In Africa, MRA incursions began at the end of World War II. Against the big anti-colonial upsurge that followed victory in 1945, MRA spent millions advocating collaboration between the forces oppressing the African peoples and those same peoples. It is not without significance that Moise Tshombe and Joseph Kasavubu of Congo (Leopoldville) are both MRA supporters. George Seldes, in his book *One Thousand Americans*, characterized MRA as a fascist organization 'subsidized by... Fascists, and with a long record of collaboration with Fascists the world over....' This description is supported by the active participation in MRA of people like General Carpentier, former commander of NATO land forces, and General Ho Ying-chin, one of Chiang Kai-shek's top generals. To cap this, several newspapers, some of them in the Western world, have claimed that MRA is actually subsidized by the CIA.

UDI AND NEO-COLONIALISM

When MRA's influence began to fail, some new instrument to cover the ideological arena was desired. It came in the establishment of the American Peace Corps in 1961 by President John Kennedy, with Sargent Shriver, Jr., his brother-in-law, in charge. Shriver, a millionaire who made his pile in land speculation in Chicago, was also known as the friend, confidant and co-worker of the former head of the Central Intelligence Agency, Allen Dulles. These two had worked together in both the Office of Strategic Services, US war-time intelligence agency, and in the CIA.

Shriver's record makes a mockery of President Kennedy's alleged instruction to Shriver to 'keep the CIA out of the Peace Corps'. So does the fact that, although the Peace Corps is advertised as a voluntary organization, all its members are carefully screened by the US Federal Bureau of Investigation (FBI).

Since its creation in 1961, members of the Peace Corps have been exposed and expelled from many African, Middle Eastern and Asian countries for acts of subversion or prejudice. Indonesia, Tanzania, the Philippines, and even pro-West countries like Turkey and Iran, have complained of its activities.

However, perhaps the chief executor of US psychological warfare is the United States Information Agency (USIA). Even for the wealthiest nation on earth, the US lavishes an unusual amount of men, materials and money on this vehicle for its neo-colonial aims.

The USIA is staffed by some 12,000 persons to the tune of more than $130 million a year. It has more than seventy editorial staffs working on publications abroad. Of its network comprising 110 radio stations, 60 are outside the US. Programmes are broadcast for Africa by American stations in Morocco, Eritrea, Liberia, Crete, and Barcelona, Spain, as well as from off-shore stations on American ships. In Africa alone, the USIA transmits about thirty territorial and national radio programmes whose content glorifies the US while attempting to discredit countries with an independent foreign policy.

The USIA boasts more than 120 branches in about 100 countries, 50 of which are in Africa alone. It has 250 centres in foreign countries, each of which is usually associated with a library. It employs about 200 cinemas and 8,000 projectors which draw upon its nearly 300 film libraries.

This agency is directed by a central body which operates in the name of the US President, planning and co-ordinating its activities in close touch with the Pentagon, CIA and other Cold War agencies, including even armed forces intelligence centres.

In developing countries, the USIA actively tries to prevent expansion of national media of information so as to capture itself the market-place of ideas. It spends huge sums for publication and distribution of about sixty newspapers and magazines in Africa, Asia and Latin America. The American government backs the USIA through direct pressures on developing nations. To ensure its agency a complete monopoly in propaganda, for instance, many agreements for economic co-operation offered by the US include a demand that Americans be granted preferential rights to disseminate information. At the same time, in trying to close the new nations to other sources of information, it employs other pressures. For instance, after agreeing to set up USIA information centres in their countries, both Togo and Congo (Leopoldville) originally hoped to follow a non-aligned path and permit Russian information centres as a balance. But Washington threatened to stop all aid, thereby forcing these two countries to renounce their plan.

Unbiased studies of the USIA by such authorities as Dr R. Holt of Princeton University, Retired Colonel R. Van de Velde, former intelligence agents Murril Dayer, Wilson Dizard, and others, have all called attention to the close ties between this agency and US Intelligence. Far example, Deputy Director Donald M. Wilson was a political intelligence agent in the US Army. Assistant Director for Europe, Joseph Philips, was a successful espionage agent in several Eastern European countries.

Some USIA duties further expose its nature as a top intelligence arm of the US imperialists. In the first place, it is expected to analyse the situation in each country, making recommendations to its Embassy, thereby to its Government, about changes that can tip the local balance in US favour. Secondly, it organizes networks of monitors for radio broadcasts and telephone conversations, while recruiting informers from government offices. It also hires people to distribute US propaganda. Thirdly, it collects secret information with special reference to defence and economy, as a means of eliminating its international military and economic competitors. Fourthly, it buys its way into local publications to influence their policies, of which Latin America furnishes numerous examples. It has been active in bribing public figures, for example in Kenya and Tunisia. Finally, it finances, directs and often supplies with arms all anti-neutralist forces in the developing countries witness Tshombe in Congo (Leopoldville) and Pak Hung Ji in South Korea. In a word, with virtually unlimited finances, there seems no bounds to its inventiveness in subversion.

One of the most recent developments in neo-colonialist strategy is the suggested establishment of a Businessmen Corps which will, like the Peace Corps, act in developing countries. In an article on 'US Intelligence and the Monopolies' in *International Affairs* (Moscow, January 1965), V. Chernyavsky writes: 'There can hardly be any doubt that this Corps is a new US intelligence organization created on the initiative of the American monopolies to use Big Business for espionage.'

It is by no means unusual for US Intelligence to set up its own business firms which are merely thinly disguised espionage centres. For example, according to Chernyavsky, the CIA has set up a firm in Taiwan known as Western Enterprises Inc. Under this cover it sends spies and saboteurs to South China. The New Asia Trading Company, a CIA firm in India, has also helped to camouflage US intelligence agents operating in Southeast Asia.

Such is the catalogue of neo-colonialism's activities and methods in our time. Upon reading it, the faint-hearted might come to fed that they must give up in despair before such an array of apparent power and seemingly inexhaustible resources.

Fortunately, however, history furnishes innumerable proofs of one of its own major laws: that the budding future is *always* stronger than the withering past. This has been amply demonstrated during every major revolution throughout history.

The American Revolution of 1776 struggled through to victory over a tangle of inefficiency, mismanagement, corruption, outright subversion and counter-revolution the likes of which has been repeated to some degree in every subsequent revolution to date.

The Russian Revolution during the period of Intervention, 1917 to 1922, appeared to be dying on its feet. The Chinese Revolution at one time was forced to pull out of its existing bases, lock stock and barrel, and make the unprecedented Long March; yet it triumphed. Imperialist white mercenaries who dropped so confidently out of the skies on Stanleyville after a plane trip from Ascension Island thought that their job would be 'duck soup'. Yet, till now, the nationalist forces of Congo (Leopoldville) continue to fight their way forward. They do not talk of *if* they will win, but only of *when*.

Asia provides a further example of the strength of a people's will to determine their own future. In South Vietnam 'special warfare' is being fought to hold back the tide of revolutionary change. 'Special warfare' is a concept of General Maxwell Taylor and a military extension of the creed of John Foster Dulles: let Asians fight Asians. Briefly, the technique is for the foreign power to supply the money, aircraft, military equipment of all kinds, and the strategic and tactical command from a General Staff down to officer 'advisers', while the troops of the puppet government bear the brunt of the fighting. Yet in spite of bombing raids and the immense build-up of foreign strength in the area, the people of both North and South Vietnam are proving to be unconquerable.

In other parts of Asia, in Cambodia, Laos, Indonesia, and now the Philippines, Thailand and Burma, the peoples of ex-colonial countries have stood firm and are winning battles against the allegedly superior imperialist enemy. In Latin America, despite 'final' punitive expeditions, the growing armed insurrections in Colombia, Venezuela and other countries continue to consolidate gains.

In Africa, we in Ghana have withstood all efforts by imperialism and its agents; Tanzania has nipped subversive plots in the bud, as have Brazzaville, Uganda and Kenya. The struggle rages back and forth. The surging popular forces may still be hampered by colonialist legacies, but nonetheless they advance inexorably.

All these examples prove beyond doubt that neo-colonialism is *not* a sign of imperialism's strength but rather of its last hideous gasp. It testifies to its inability to rule any longer by old methods. Independence is a luxury it can no longer afford to permit its subject peoples, so that even what it claims to have 'given' it now seeks to take away.

This means that neo-colonialism *can* and *will* be defeated. How can this be done?

Thus far, all the methods of neo-colonialists have pointed in one direction, the ancient, accepted one of all minority ruling classes throughout history – *divide and rule.*

Quite obviously, therefore, *unity* is the first requisite for destroying neo-colonialism. Primary and basic is the need for an all-union government on the much divided continent of Africa. Along with that, a strengthening of the Afro-Asian Solidarity Organization and the spirit of Bandung is already under way. To it, we must seek the adherence on an increasingly formal basis of our Latin American brothers.

Furthermore, all these liberatory forces have, on all major issues and at every possible instance, the support of the growing socialist sector of the world.

Finally, we must encourage and utilize to the full those still all too few yet growing instances of support for liberation and anti-colonialism inside the imperialist world itself.

UDI AND NEO-COLONIALISM

To carry out such a political programme, we must all back it with national plans designed to strengthen ourselves as independent nations. An external condition for such independent development is neutrality or *political non-alignment*. This has been expressed in two conferences of Non-Aligned Nations during the recent past, the last of which, in Cairo in 1964, clearly and inevitably showed itself at one with the rising forces of liberation and human dignity.

And the preconditions for all this, to which lip service is often paid but activity seldom directed, is to develop ideological clarity among the anti-imperialist, anti-colonialist, pro-liberation masses of our continents. They, and they alone, make, maintain or break revolutions.

With the utmost speed, neo-colonialism must be analysed in clear and simple terms for the full mass understanding by the surging organizations of the African peoples. The All-African Trade Union Federation (AATUF) has already made a start in this direction, while the Pan-African Youth Movement, the women, journalists, farmers and others are not far behind. Bolstered with ideological clarity, these organizations, closely linked with the ruling parties where liberatory forces are in power, will prove that neo-colonialism is the symptom of imperialism's weakness and that it is defeatable. For, when all is said and done, it is the so-called little man, the bent-backed, exploited, malnourished, blood-covered fighter for independence who decides. And he invariably decides for freedom.

CONCLUSION

In the Introduction, I attempted to set out the dilemma now facing the world. The conflict between rich and poor in the second half of the nineteenth century and the first half of the twentieth, which was fought out between the rich and the poor in the developed nations of the world ended in a compromise. Capitalism as a system disappeared from large areas of the world, but where socialism was established it was in its less developed rather than its more developed parts and, in fact, the revolt against capitalism had its greatest successes in those areas where early neo-colonialism had been most actively practised. In the industrially more developed countries, capitalism, far from disappearing, became infinitely stronger. This strength was only achieved by the sacrifice of two principles which had inspired early capitalism, namely the subjugation of the working classes within each individual country and the exclusion of the State from any say in the control of capitalist enterprise.

By abandoning these two principles and substituting for them 'welfare states' based on high working-class living standards and on a State-regulated capitalism at home, the developed countries succeeded in exporting their internal problem and transferring the conflict between rich and poor from the national to the international stage.

Marx had argued that the development of capitalism would produce a crisis within each individual capitalist State because within each State the gap between the 'haves' and the 'have nots' would widen to a point where a conflict was inevitable and that it would be the capitalists who would be defeated. The basis of his argument is not invalidated by the fact that the conflict, which he had predicted as a national one, did not everywhere take place on a national scale but has been transferred instead to the world stage. World capitalism has postponed its crisis but only at the cost of transforming it into an international crisis. The danger is now not civil war within individual States provoked by intolerable conditions within those States, but international war provoked ultimately by the misery of the majority of mankind who daily grow poorer and poorer.

When Africa becomes economically free and politically united, the monopolists will come face to face with their own working class in their own countries, and a new struggle will arise within which the liquidation and collapse of imperialism will be complete.

As this book has attempted to show, in the same way as the internal crisis of capitalism within the developed world arose through the uncontrolled action of national capital, so a greater crisis is being provoked today by similar uncontrolled action of international capitalism in the developing parts of the world. Before the problem can be solved it must at least be understood. It cannot be resolved merely by pretending that neo-colonialism does not exist. It must be realized that the methods at present employed to solve the problem of world poverty are not likely to yield any result other than to extend the crisis.

Speaking in 1951, the then President of the United States, Mr Truman, said, 'The only kind of war we seek is the good old fight against man's ancient enemies ... poverty, disease, hunger and illiteracy.' Sentiments of a similar nature have been re-echoed by all political leaders in the developed world but the stark fact remains: whatever wars may have been won since 1951, none of them is the war against poverty, disease, hunger and illiteracy. However little other types of war have been deliberately sought, they are the only ones which have been waged. Nothing is gained by assuming that those who express such views are insincere. The position of the leaders of the developed capitalist countries of the world are, in relation to the great neo-colonialist international financial combines, very similar to that which Lord Macaulay described as existing between the directors of the East India Company and their agent, Warren Hastings, who, in the eighteenth century, engaged in the wholesale plunder of India. Macaulay wrote:

> 'The Directors, it is true, never enjoined or applauded any crime. Far from it. Whoever examines their letters written at the time will find there are many just and humane sentiments, many excellent precepts, in short, an admirable code of political ethics. But each exultation is modified or nullified by a demand for money. ...We by no means accuse or suspect those who framed these dispatches of hypocrisy. It is probable that, written 15,000 miles from the place where their orders were to be carried into effect, they never perceived the gross inconsistency of which they were guilty. But the inconsistency was at once manifest to their lieutenant in Calcutta.... Hastings saw that it was absolutely necessary for him to disregard either the moral discourses or the pecuniary requisitions of his employers. Being forced to disobey them in something, he had to consider what kind of disobedience they would most readily pardon; and he correctly judged that the safest course would be to neglect the sermons and to find the rupees.'

Today the need both to maintain a welfare state, i.e. a parasite State at home, and to support a huge and ever-growing burden of armament costs makes it absolutely essential for developed capitalist countries to secure the maximum return in profit from such parts of the international financial complex as they control. However much private capitalism is exhorted to bring about rapid development and a rising standard of living in the less developed areas of the world, those who manipulate the system realize the inconsistency between doing this and producing at the same time the funds necessary to maintain the sinews of war and the welfare state at home. They know when it comes to the issue they will be excused if they fail to provide for a world-wide rise in the standard of living. They know they will never be forgiven if they betray the system and produce a crisis at home which either destroys the affluent State or interferes with its military preparedness.

Appeals to capitalism to work out a cure for the division of the world into rich and poor are likely to have no better result than the appeals of the Directors of the East India Company to Warren Hastings to ensure social justice in India. Faced with a choice, capitalism, like Hastings, will come down on the side of exploitation.

Is there then no method of avoiding the inevitable world conflict occasioned by an international class war? To accept that world conflict is inevitable is to reject any belief in co-existence or in the policy of non-alignment as practised at present by many of the countries attempting to escape from neo colonialism. A way out is possible.

To start with, for the first time in human history the potential material resources of the world are so great that there is no need for there to be rich and poor. It is only the organization to deploy these potential resources that is lacking. Effective world pressure can force such a redeployment, but world pressure is not exercised by appeals, however eloquent, or by arguments, however convincing. It is only achieved by deeds. It is necessary to secure a world realignment so that those who are at the moment the helpless victims of a system will be able in the future to exert a counter pressure. Such counter pressures do not lead to war. On the contrary, it is often their absence which constitutes the threat to peace.

A parallel can be drawn with the methods by which direct colonialism was ended. No imperial power has ever granted independence to a colony unless the forces were such that no other course was possible, and there are many instances where independence was only achieved by a war of liberation, but there are many other instances when no such war occurred. The very organization of the forces of independence within the colony was sufficient to convince the imperial power that resistance to independence would be impossible or that the political and economic consequences of a colonial war outweighed any advantage to be gained by retaining the colony.

In the earlier chapters of this book I have set out the argument for African unity and have explained how this unity would destroy neo-colonialism in Africa. In later chapters I have explained how strong is the world position of those who profit from neo-colonialism. Nevertheless, African unity is something which is within the grasp of the African people. The foreign firms who exploit our resources long ago saw the strength to be gained from acting on a Pan-African scale. By means of interlocking directorships, cross-shareholdings and other devices, groups of apparently different companies have formed, in fact, one enormous capitalist monopoly. The only effective way to challenge this economic empire and to recover possession of our heritage, is for us also to act an a Pan-African basis, through a Union Government.

UDI AND NEO-COLONIALISM

No one would suggest that if all the peoples of Africa combined to establish their unity their decision could be revoked by the forces of neo-colonialism. On the contrary, faced with a new situation, those who practise neo-colonialism would adjust themselves to this new balance of world forces in exactly the same way as the capitalist world has in the past adjusted itself to any other change in the balance of power.

The danger to world peace springs not from the action of those who seek to end neo-colonialism but from the inaction of those who allow it to continue. To argue that a third world war is not inevitable is one thing, to suppose that it can be avoided by shutting our eyes to the development of a situation likely to produce it is quite another matter.

If world war is not to occur it must be prevented by positive action. This positive action is within the power of the peoples of those areas of the world which now suffer under neo-colonialism but it is only within their power if they act at once, with resolution and in unity.

INDEX

Accra xiv, 1, 3, 5, 11, 36, 118, 121, 170, 172
Addis Ababa 5, 8, 29, 46, 47, 64, 70, 71, 72, 117, 121, 123
Africa Day Special Message by Kwame Nkrumah 159
Africa Must Unite 150, 151, 152
African Affairs Centre, Accra 3
African Development Bank 71
African High Command 5, 96, 117, 126, 166
Afro-Asian Solidarity Organisation 194
Aid Agency for International Development 170, 179, 181-183, 185-186, 188, 189
Algeria(n) 157, 177, 184, 189
All African Government 171, 194, 198
All African Peoples Conference, Accra, 1958 7, 11
All African Trade Union Federation (AATUF) 195
All-African Union Government 6, 71, 119, 124, 154, 166, 171, 194, 198
American Federsation of Labor (AFL) 187
Angola, Republic of 40, 66, 94, 137
Apartheid 11
Armah, Kwesi 120
Ascension Island 193

Asia, Asians 10, 15, 131, 172, 180, 183, 185-188, 190-192, 194
Australia 113, 181
Austria 113, 188
Axioms by Kwame Nkrumah vii, 149, 150

Beadle, Sir Hugh 76, 85, 88
Bechuanaland, Rep. of 66
Bottomley, Arther 59, 60, 62
Britain, Great 118
British South African Company xi, 7, 9, 10, 18, 21, 30
Bulawayo 50
Bureau of African Affairs, Accra 3
Buttler, R.A. 41, 45, 47

Cairo 71, 72, 105, 195
Cambodia 183-5, 194
Canada 181
Caribbean 183
Central African Conference (1963) 35, 47, 48
Central African Federation (CAF), 1953 10, 14, 24, 40, 49, 122
Central Intelligence Agency (CIA) 183, 187, 189-191, 193
Ceylon 185
Challenge of the Congo by Kwame Nkrumah 154
Chiang Kai-Shek 180, 190

INDEX

China, Chinese 156
Class Struggle in Africa by Kwame Nkrumah 14
Cold War 191
Columbia 194
Commonwealth 55, 79, 80, 81, 82, 83, 86, 87, 91, 120
Commonwealth Prime Ministers Conference, London (1964) 57
Commonwealth Prime Ministers Conference London (1965) 60
Commonwealth Secretariat 124
Communism(ist) 178, 181, 184, 186, 189
Conakry, Capital of Rep. of Guinea 2, 145, 149, 150
Conference of Independent African States, Accra 1958 7
Congo (Brazzaville) 37, 97, 194
Congo (Leopoldville) (Zaire) (Kinshasa) 1, 96, 97, 116, 164, 174, 184, 190, 192-3
Convention People's Party (CPP) xvi, 2, 3, 5, 11, 136, 145
Costa Rica 189
Crete 191
Cuba(an) 3, 184
Cyprus 40, 132, 184, 189

Dean, Sir Patrick 46
De Gaulle 146, 183-4
Devonshire Declaration (1923) 8, 10, 52, 54, 106
Dulles, Allen 191
Dulles, John Foster 51, 194
Dupont, C.W. xv, 89, 112

Egypt, Rep. of (& United Arab Rep.) 37, 39, 40, 174
East European Countries 186, 192
Eire (Ireland) 181
England (see Britain) 177, 181, 183
Eritrea 191
Europe, Europeans 181, 183, 192

Executive Council of the OAU 64, 65, 166

Far East(ern) 177, 180
Federal Bureau of Investigation (FBI) 191
Federation of Rhodesia and Nyasaland xii, 10, 24
Field, Wiston 28, 39, 42, 46, 47, 54, 56, 57
Finland 180
Formosa 184
France, French 89, 119, 128, 146, 174, 177
Frank, Prof. Thomas 38

Gabon 183
Gardiner, Lord 59, 60
Germany, German 184
Ghana, Rep. of 97, 99, 170-172, 175, 189, 194
Gibbs, Sir Humphrey 88, 140
Gold Coast (see Ghana)
Gonakudzingwa (Camp) 60
Greece 181, 184
Guatamala 184
Guinea, Rep. of 2, 96, 97, 99

Handbook of Revolutionary Warfare by Kwame Nkrumah 2, 6, 149, 153, 155
Hansard 45, 53
Hirsch, Dr. M.I. 60
Hitler, Adolf 122
Hobson, Sir John 32
Home, Alex Douglas 58
Hughes, Cledwyn 62
Hungary 184

I Speak of Freedom by Kwame Nkrumah 150
India 67, 193, 197-8
International Confederation of Free Trade Union (ICFTU) 188

201

INDEX

International Monetary Fund (IMF) 180-181, 185
Invisible Government, The 171, 183-4, 190
Iran 184, 191
Iraq 184
Ireland (see Eire) 181
Italy 183

Johnson (President) 171
Johovah's Witness 189
Japan (Japanese) 39, 181, 183
Jawara, Dawda 61, 66

Kasavubu, Joseph 190
Kataknga 14, 29, 45, 95, 107
Kaunda, Kenneth 47, 61, 87, 94, 168
Kennedy, John (President) 191
Kenya, Rep. of 34, 132, 188, 192, 194
Kenyatta, Jomo 89

Labour Party (British) 78, 81, 110, 146, 187-8
Lagos Conference 136
Land Apportionment Act 109, 131, 138
Laos 184, 194
Latin American (South America) 172, 181, 183, 185, 192, 194
Liberia 191
Lo Bengula (Lobengula) 9, 17, 105, 106
Long March 193
Lumumba, Patrice 159

Macdonald, Malcom 94
Malawi, Rep. of 85, 103, 106, 107
Mashonaland 9, 18, 105
Matabele (People) 9, 17, 18
Matabeleland 9, 105
Marx, Karl 180, 196
Middle East(ern) 181, 186, 191
Monckton Commission 32, 33, 44
Moral Re-Armament (MRA) 190-1

Morocco 36, 37, 108, 191
Motion of Destiny Speech 150, 151
Mozambique, Rep. of 42, 43, 66, 95, 102, 103, 104, 137, 160, 161

Namibia (see S.W. Africa) 64, 66
Neo-colonialism by Kwame Nkrumah 1, 7, 104, 151, 169-199
New Zealand 27, 113, 181
Nigeria, Rep. of (Nigerian) 69, 188, 189
Nkomo Jushua 60, 74, 77, 81, 83
Nkrumah, Kwame 1, 2, 3, 61, 65, 78, 84, 89, 94, 99, 118, 120, 136-7, 145, 146, 149
Non-Alignment Nations 195
North Atlantic Treaty Organisation (NATO) 190-1
Northern Rhodesia 10, 24, 25
Nyasaland 10, 25, 44, 45, 48, 53, 107
Nyerere Julius 61, 71, 89

OAU 4, 5, 63, 64, 65, 68, 69, 70, 72, 73, 74, 172
OAU Summit, Addis Ababa (1964) 120
OAU Summit Accra (1965) 65, 73, 77, 90, 172
Oboto, Milton 61, 89
One Man One Vote 76, 77
Organisation of African Unity (see also OAU) 63, 64, 65, 68, 69, 70, 72, 73, 74, 89, 91, 92, 96, 101, 158, 172

Pan-African(ism)(nist) 2, 11, 64, 145, 157
Panaf Books 2, 8, 145, 149
Peace Corps 170, 189-191, 193
Pentagon 183, 189, 191
Philippines 191, 194
Poland 184
Portugal, Portuguese 42, 91, 125, 128, 129, 134-5, 140, 159, 183
Positive Action 152, 199

INDEX

Revolutionary Path by Kwame Nkrumah 64, 149
Rhodes, Cecil 7, 17, 105
Rhodesia and Nyasaland Act (1963) 24, 48
Rhodesian Front Party 2, 7, 95, 108, 140, 143
Ribeiro, Miguel Augustus 170
Rome 190

Sahara 183
Salisbury (Harare) 1, 2, 9
Second World War 11, 39, 183-4, 190
Security Council, UN 37, 90, 91
Sekou Toure Ahmed 2, 4, 99, 121, 145, 146
Shriver, Sargent 191
Sithole, Rev. N. 57, 74, 81
Smith, Ian 14, 27, 28, 29, 57, 58, 59, 62, 88, 91, 108, 123, 130, 141, 147, 158
South Africa, Rep. of (Union of) 98, 102, 103, 108, 133, 181
Southern Rhodesia 14, 96, 99, 101, 107, 130, 131, 133
Stanleyville (Kisangani) 193
Suez 108, 184

Taiwan 193
Tanzania, Rep. of 61, 96, 97, 119, 191, 194
Times, The 186
Third World 189
Tobacco Marketing Board 20
Togo 69
Towards Colonial Freedom by Kwame Nkrumah 187-9
Trade Union Movement (Union, Unions, Unionists) 187-9
Treaty of Mutual Defence and Security 5, 94, 97, 129
Truman, Harray 196
Tshombe, Moise 190, 192

Tunisia 192
Turkey 184, 191

UDI 4, 6, 58, 59, 60, 61, 62, 63, 88, 89, 90, 93, 94, 137, 138, 143, 169
Uganda, Rep. of 89, 96, 97
Unilateral Declaration of Independence (UDI) see UDI 74, 75, 169
United Kingdom 90, 91, 92, 98, 100, 101, 102
United Nations (UN/UNO) 93, 98, 100, 102, 103, 182, 187
UN Security Council 75, 93, 103
USSR 184, 186, 193
USA 170, 171, 174, 180, 184, 185, 192, 198

Venezuela 194
Victoria Falls Conference 35, 45, 47
Vienna 190
Vietnam, Vietnamise 1, 67

Wall Street Journal (The) 180-2
Ward, Barbara 181
Washington, D.C. 192
Welensky, Sir Roy 7, 41
Whitehead, Sir Edgar 7, 28
Williams, Mennen 170, 171
Wilson, Harald 63, 77, 78, 83, 84, 118, 122, 123, 146
World Bank 170, 185-6
World Fed. of Trade Union (WFTU) 187

Zanzibar 28
Zambia, Rep. of 7, 102, 103, 105, 107, 115, 126
Zimbabwe, Rep. of 2, 4, 6, 7, 117, 126
Zimbabwe African National Union (ZANU) 6, 25, 57
Zimbabwe African People's Union (ZAPU) 6, 25, 109, 110

www.ingramcontent.com/pod-product-compliance
Lightning Source LLC
Chambersburg PA
CBHW051357290426
44108CB00015B/2049